PUBLICATIONS OF THE BUREAU OF BUSINESS
AND ECONOMIC RESEARCH

UNIVERSITY OF CALIFORNIA, LOS ANGELES

Previously published in this series:

THE NATURE OF COMPETITION IN GASOLINE DISTRIBUTION AT
THE RETAIL LEVEL
by Ralph Cassady, Jr., and Wylie L. Jones (1951)

THE PACIFIC COAST MARITIME SHIPPING INDUSTRY, 1930–1948
VOLUME I: AN ECONOMIC PROFILE
By Wytze Gorter and George H. Hildebrand (1952)

THE ROLE OF MERGERS IN THE GROWTH OF LARGE FIRMS
by J. Fred Weston (1953)

THE PACIFIC COAST MARITIME SHIPPING INDUSTRY, 1930–1948
VOLUME II: AN ANALYSIS OF PERFORMANCE
by Wytze Gorter and George H. Hildebrand (1954)

THE MEXICAN PETROLEUM INDUSTRY, 1930–1958
by J. Richard Powell (1956)

THE PERSECUTION OF HUGUENOTS AND FRENCH ECONOMIC DEVELOPMENT,
1680–1720
by Warren C. Scoville (1960)

"Disguised Unemployment"
in Underdeveloped Areas

with special reference to
South Korean Agriculture

PUBLICATIONS OF THE BUREAU OF BUSINESS AND ECONOMIC RESEARCH
UNIVERSITY OF CALIFORNIA, LOS ANGELES

"Disguised Unemployment" in Underdeveloped Areas

with special reference to

South Korean Agriculture

BY YONG SAM CHO

UNIVERSITY OF CALIFORNIA PRESS

Berkeley and Los Angeles 1963

UNIVERSITY OF CALIFORNIA PRESS
BERKELEY AND LOS ANGELES

CAMBRIDGE UNIVERSITY PRESS
LONDON, ENGLAND

To My Mother

WITH DEEPEST RESPECT

AND LOVE

Preface

The purpose of this book is to examine the most respected concepts and theories on surplus labor in underdeveloped agricultural economics, particularly in the literature on "disguised unemployment," and to point out their flaws. This leaves the way clear toward finding a more valid concept and theory on this vital subject, which is the core of potential economic and social development in backward countries.

After establishing a more realistic and workable definition of surplus labor, on the basis of a closer investigation of the extended family-clan-village system, so typical of tradition-guided underdeveloped societies, we proceed to work out a method for measuring true surplus labor, with rural Korea as an example. Because of the unavoidable distinction between technical (open) idle labor and tradition-directed (closed) idle labor, the measuring of true surplus labor becomes quite involved and requires considerable thought and much vigilance. In this study a new method for estimating farm surplus labor, which has not yet been applied, is used.

Having obtained quantitative data on the extent of underemployment in the sample country, we continue with a discussion of policy implications in the employment structure of underdeveloped countries, as we see them, and construct a proposed program for the utilization of true surplus labor without applying totalitarian methods, without waiting for the availability of additional capital from outside the agricultural community, and without making a change in traditional institutions as an a priori condition for the utilization of idle labor.

Our program calls for capital improvements within the agricultural area, financed by the agricultural sector itself, after we show, through statistical data, that capital improvements in agriculture yield quicker and greater results than do similar capital investments in other sectors of the economy. We also attempt to show how such a program would not only put to work a major part of unutilized labor on agricultural development projects, but would pave the way toward a gradual dissolution of those social traditions and institutions that have been economically hampering and that have been, consequently, an important cause of perpetuating economic and social stagnation.

For financing these capital development projects we make specific proposals. We propose to make better use of government subsidies given to individual farmers in order to improve farm facilities and encourage production. The scheme is to use the fund in a lump sum for community projects. We also advocate a land rent tax to retain some of the net land rent paid to absentee landowners. If properly carried out, this measure could be regarded as a desirable substitute for land reform.

In order to improve the present rural economy, we propose to replace the present land income tax with a land property tax. The same total revenue could be collected from a tax on land instead of on income, without adversely affecting incremental output. The land income tax discriminates against those who produce more per unit of land (e.g., the farmers with small holdings).

We claim for our program the added advantage of minimizing social unrest that results from economic distress or from an imposed change in prevailing traditions and institutions, thus safeguarding political stability within the framework of needed and planned reforms. It is partly with this in view and partly to obviate the need for chronically unavailable additional capital that we have conducted our inquiry and formulated our program largely within the constraints of the *ceteris paribus* assumption.

This study would have been impossible without the coöperation of the South Korean government. I wish to thank the research departments of the Bank of Korea and the Korean Agricultural Bank, the departments of Finance and of Agriculture and Forestry of the Republic of Korea, and the Korean Consulate General in

Los Angeles. Special thanks are due to Mr. Hong Yoon-Sup, assistant manager of the Research Department of the Bank of Korea, who directed much of the statistical work, and whose answers to many questions were indispensable to this study. A special acknowledgment is also owing to Mr. Suh Kyung Ho, manager of the Department of Research and Statistics of the Korean Agricultural Bank.

I am deeply grateful for the constant advice and help of Professor Donald E. Stout. I also owe many thanks to Professor Robert E. Baldwin, who read two drafts of this study and whose many useful comments and criticisms contributed greatly to its improvement. Professors W. Lee Hansen, Harold M. Somers, James M. Gillies, and Ralph Cassady, Jr., also made many valuable suggestions. Professor Rosenstein-Rodan of the Massachusetts Institute of Technology kindly made available to me his memorandum on the method of measuring "disguised unemployment."

I must also thank my American and Korean friends and my younger brother, Yong Sye Cho, for their editorial and typing assistance. Laura Y. C. Ho, Delaine Helms, Lee Yoon Jin, and Mrs. Miriam Morton were especially patient and helpful.

Finally, I appreciate the financial assistance made available by the University of California for research and editorial work.

All the institutions and persons to whom this study is so much indebted are truly coauthors. Needless to say, however, they are not responsible for any of the views expressed in this study, for which the author alone takes responsibility.

Los Angeles, California   YONG SAM CHO
October, 1962

Contents

sonal Fluctuations in Employment—Significance of the Difference between Casual Wage Labor and Attached Wage Labor—Differences in Underemployment of Self-supporting Family Labor and Attached Wage Labor—Measurement of Technical and Tradition-directed Underemployment—Validity of the Assumptions—Conclusion

Tables

Figures

I

The Setting

In underdeveloped countries labor is assumed to be the most abundant asset. How to make the best use of this asset has recently become a key problem in the theory and policy of economic development. Nevertheless, there is no definite analysis of this problem to be found among the numerous studies made thus far. The main purpose of this study is to reëxamine the concept of surplus labor in underdeveloped agricultural economies, and to indicate a different approach to the understanding of the many complicated aspects of manpower utilization in such economies. The scope of this book, however, extends beyond a conceptual analysis of surplus labor and of manpower utilization; an attempt is also made to measure the amount of labor which could be mobilized for alternative uses. On the basis of the policy implications derived both from the conceptual analysis and from the actual measurement of withdrawable labor, specific proposals are made which may be readily applicable without waiting for changes to take place over a period of time.

The conceptual elements of this study are essentially static. We assume that the size of the population and the amount of capital and of other technical means of production are given. What constitutes surplus labor at any given time has a clear and unequivocal meaning only when rigid constraints on the availability and the nature of technology and capital are assumed. The South Korean agricultural community is presented here as a study example. (South Korea will hereafter be referred to as Korea.) Of course, the quantitative and qualitative data on this one country will not suffice for broad generalizations applicable to underdeveloped agricultural societies whose social, economic, and political conditions differ from those in Korea. But underdeveloped agricultural societies, especially those in rice-growing regions, have, in fact, much in common. Such societies are characterized by similar agricultural patterns and social institutions, insufficiency of technical means of production, and poverty.

DISGUISED UNEMPLOYMENT CONSIDERED
AS SURPLUS LABOR

In the literature of economics, one concept of unemployment is applied to economically advanced countries and another to relatively underdeveloped countries. In economically advanced countries unemployment is, it is said, "open," implying that there are some workers who are seeking jobs but cannot find them at going wage rates. But for underdeveloped countries, particularly in agricultural areas, there is said to be a special concept of unemployment, that is, so-called "disguised unemployment." [1] According to this concept of unemployment, there are certain workers who seem to be working, but who do not thereby increase the total output; therefore, such employment of labor is regarded as being no better than no employment at all.

In current analytical terms, disguised unemployment means that, if the amount of capital stock available is more or less fixed at a very low level, the growth of population causes diminishing returns up to the point where the absorption of labor into the given capital stock reduces the marginal productivity of employed labor to zero or to near zero (or even to a negative value). Accord-

---

[1] Ragnar Nurkse, *Problems of Capital Formation in Underdeveloped Countries* (Oxford: Basil Blackwell, 1955), p. 33; International Labor Office, *The Economic Background of Social Policy, Including Problems of Industrialization*, Report IV (New Delhi, 1947), p. 148; United Nations Economic Commission for Asia and the Far East, *Economic Survey of Asia and the Far East, 1950* (New York, 1950), pp. 70–74; P. N. Rosenstein-Rodan, "Disguised Unemployment and Underemployment in Agriculture," *Monthly Bulletin of Agricultural Economics and Statistics*, VI (July-Aug., 1957), 1–5; and N. Georgescu-Roegen, "Economic Theory and Agrarian Economics," *Oxford Economic Papers*, XII (Feb., 1960), 13–14. Additional references will be found in chapter ii.

ing to this concept of unemployment, the reason such unnecessary labor is employed rests on the nature of the prevailing social institutions. In particular, the extended family system results in no visible or overt unemployment but only in the kind of unemployment that is not visible, and is said to be "disguised."

Economists assume that the existence of this "disguised" unemployment makes it possible to remove redundant labor from the farm land and apply it where its employment would be more useful, under the assumption of *ceteris paribus*.[2] It is claimed that, as some of the labor actually employed in agriculture could be dispensed with in this way, persons thus employed—that is, the disguised unemployed—can therefore be regarded as surplus labor. In other words, the terms "disguised unemployment" and "surplus labor" are used interchangeably. In this current thinking the line of causation is thus neatly ordered as follows: (1) overpopulation is assumed;[3] (2) the extended family system leads to unnecessary application of labor; (3) there appears, therefore, a special kind of full employment, meaning that all eligible persons only seem to be working; but (4) the marginal productivity of this unnecessarily applied labor is zero; and (5) this labor, having zero marginal productivity, may be dispensed with in the agricultural operation under the *ceteris paribus* assumption.

I am not satisfied with this prevailing causative series of assumptions, but differ from it in several significant ways. (1) The social institution of the extended family system—family, clan, and village—is a key cause of rural congested population (not to be mistaken for overpopulation in terms of economic productivity). This massive rural population is a preferred way of life and not only encourages large families but also attracts people back to rural living, thus further augmenting the population. (2) There is, however, no unnecessary application of labor in such communities.

---

[2] See p. 9 for a detailed discussion of this assumption.

[3] Professors Meier and Baldwin define "overpopulation" as follows: " 'Overpopulation' usually refers to a population larger than the 'optimum population'—an optimum population being defined as one that maximizes per capita output, given the other inputs and state of technology. In this sense, so long as there are increasing returns to scale in the economy, population may be less than optimum. But, after a point, as population increases, the rate of rise of output per head slows down, until eventually in conformity with the classical and neo-classical principle of diminishing returns output per head declines as population grows" (Gerald M. Meier and Robert E. Baldwin, *Economic Development: Theory, History, Policy* [New York: John Wiley & Sons, 1957], p. 281 n. 8).

(3) Therefore there is no special kind of false full employment or the entailed disguised unemployment. (4) Instead, visible under-employment, rather than disguised (or invisible) unemployment, is characteristic of underdeveloped agricultural communities to-day.[4] (5) Thus it is meaningless to talk about the marginal produc-tivity of idle labor. (6) Consequently, *ceteris paribus,* actual sur-plus labor is far less extensive than is prevalently assumed.

The defects in the prevailing views lie not so much in logical inconsistencies as in the lack of correct empirical content in their premises. To return for a moment to the matter of so-called over-population: if one takes the view that overpopulation results in the use of unnecessary labor, one implies wholesale irrationality on the part of the people of underdeveloped agricultural com-munities. Are these people really so irrational as habitually to apply labor unnecessarily? It is difficult to reconcile this view with the indisputable facts of low caloric intake and of physical and mental fatigue associated with agricultural work (see chap. ii). It is also difficult to justify this view without providing for substan-tial changes in agricultural organization, technology, and capital, which would provide additional work (see chap. vi).

GENERAL CAUSES OF UNDEREMPLOYMENT

The concept of disguised unemployment ignores a most vivid fact of rural life in underdeveloped agricultural communities—the existence of part-time overt idle labor. Not all farm workers in underdeveloped agricultural communities are actually working at any one time. Because the family unit is large, all its members may be partially employed (i.e., underemployed), particularly in off seasons.[5]

Underemployment in such communities is usually caused by many deep-rooted factors, which, for purposes of analysis, may be classified into technical factors and social factors. Technical factors include the scarcity of capital (including land) and technology relative to the growth of the work force; the inelasticity of the demand for and the supply of native commodities; and the system

---

[4] For definitions of "underemployment" and "unemployment" see pp. 7–8 and n. 6, below.

[5] See p. 7 for the definition of "family."

of production. A notable example of a technical factor is the seasonal nature of agricultural operation. Social factors include customs and tradition, and attitudes toward knowledge, invention, and enterprise. All such social institutions may reduce the strength of economic motivation and impede the mobility of resources, and consequently may lead to underemployment.

The phenomenon of underemployment is not unique in underdeveloped countries. It may also exist in economically advanced countries as a result of the technical and social factors cited above, but there, presumably, it exerts less economic impact. Let us consider, for example, the picture of farm employment in the United States, where underemployment of farmers is partly technical and partly traditional. Because social institutions (along with technical conditions) in underdeveloped agricultural communities are not necessarily unique to them, it would hardly appear necessary to devise a special kind of concept—that is, the concept of disguised unemployment—to distinguish between underemployment in economically underdeveloped areas and underemployment in economically advanced areas.

AN ALTERNATIVE APPROACH

What meaning, then, can the term "disguised" possibly have? The answer springs directly from the preceding analysis of underemployment. The term "disguised" can be applied only to underemployment caused by social factors, not to that caused by technical factors. In other words, social factors in underdeveloped agricultural communities, such as customs and tradition, may be taken as relevant to the meaning of "disguised." These social institutions assign special values to work, to unregimented village life, and to relatively riskless or secure rural life. The value attached to the traditional way of life is one of the important reasons for enlarging the size of the family unit and thus increasing the volume of self-supporting family labor. That the self-supporting family laborer always enjoys rural life is, however, not meant in an absolute sense (i.e., his life may be ridden with hunger and disease), but in a relative sense—relative because, in an economy where the range of choice is greatly limited, the value attached to the income

from self-employment, plus the value attached to rural life generally, exceeds the value accruing to any available alternative. These
people are presumably not happy in material terms, but not unhappy enough to break away from the traditional social values.
Under these circumstances idle labor reflects the value placed
upon social institutions rather than reflecting technical factors.
Ceteris paribus, such idle labor is not permanently withdrawable
from the land for economic development unless a totalitarian
method is used; therefore it is not true surplus labor in the usual
sense (see chap. v). This idle labor may be termed "tradition-
directed underemployment." We shall, for convenience, refer to
this as "closed" (or "voluntary") underemployment. This analysis suggests that if the term "disguised" has any plausible meaning, it must signify this type of tradition-directed behavior on the
part of self-supporting laborers.

But the problem of underemployment is not wholly tradition-
directed. Regardless of the type of social organization, overt idle
labor exists because of the insufficiency of all technical means of
production (including land), and this labor, in many agricultural
economies, appears in the form of seasonal and/or chronic idle
labor. These types of idle labor exist in different types of social
organization. When idle labor is chronic, it is true surplus labor
in the sense that it can be removed from the land permanently
for an alternative use, under the *ceteris paribus* assumption (see
chap. v). Idle labor due to an insufficiency of technical means of
production is called "technical underemployment" or "open" (or
"involuntary") underemployment.

From the standpoint of economic policy, it would be useful to
differentiate one kind of underemployment from the other—that
is, closed (voluntary) underemployment from open (involuntary)
underemployment—as to volume. An approach to the approxi-
mation of each type of underemployment without precise personal
identification of the underemployed is shown in chapter v. The
basic ideas in the procedure are: (1) wage laborers (landless laborers) in a tradition-directed society are marginal individuals who,
lacking the advantages and the prestige of landownership, are not
committed to or involved in the *status quo,* and are not employed
in the tradition-directed sense; (2) the extent of employment of
wage laborers, who are as fully employed as is possible, is used to

measure the two kinds of underemployment. In other words, the extent of employment of these wage laborers collectively serves as a yardstick for the measurement (see chap. v for detailed explanations and the actual application of this method).

DEFINITION OF BASIC TERMS: FAMILY, UNDEREMPLOYMENT, *CETERIS PARIBUS*

It is appropriate here to be explicit about certain definitions. The word "family" is usually defined as a household with a common kitchen, living under the same roof, and including temporary absentees but excluding guests. A farm family in a traditional society tends to embrace more than one unit of monogenic parents and their children. It may include members related by common descent or marriage, as well as servants.

Because of the analytical purpose of this study, and because of empirical evidence, the family is defined in a different way. A household may consist of self-supporting family members and attached wageworkers; the former may be further classified as farm-owning family members or nonfarm-owning family members. The nonfarm-owning family members may be other than the family members of direct descent. The nonlandowning family members work not as employees but as members of the family, and receive their share of the total output resulting from the joint labor. They are usually close relatives of farm owners, but they often live in separate dwellings. Although the attached wage laborer lives with the employer's family, he is actually a hired worker who receives a wage, usually on annual contract; he does not automatically receive his share of the family output although he may be a distant relative of the self-supporting family members. This kinship is too distant to eliminate the relationship of employer and employee.

In this study, therefore, a family is a unit in which members work together and share the joint product according to need, regardless of whether or not they live under one roof. It is a fact of deep-rooted tradition that the status of family membership does not depend on living under one roof. The family, as here defined, embraces nonfarm-owning family laborers who may own separate quarters and kitchens, but it does not include attached wageworkers. The automatic sharing of the joint product is the crucial criterion in defining the family.

"Underemployment" exists when the full number of labor hours available is not being utilized, and when there is part-time employment in the usual sense. In many underdeveloped agricultural economies characterized by small-scale family farming and traditional value systems, underemployment is more likely to prevail than unemployment.[6] The use of the concept of unemployment in this connection is somewhat misleading, as it is more often used in connection with wageworkers whose status is thus recorded in unemployment statistics. I prefer to use the less precise

---

[6] The definition of "unemployment" has always been arbitrary. Unemployment census data cannot be used here because we need the number of hours of unemployment for a given period of time (i.e., for a day, a month, or a year), not the number of persons unemployed on any given census day or census week. It may be instructive, for instance, to show what the United States census does with unemployment statistics. The Bureau of the Census makes a completely arbitrary distinction between total lack of work and partial lack of work. The present concept of unemployment understates the true level of joblessness because it excludes the partially unemployed; it classifies part-time workers and those involuntarily working less than a full workweek as employed. On the other hand, when unemployables, ne'er-do-wells, floaters, and the like are reported as looking for work, they are counted as unemployed. Their inclusion overstates the level of joblessness.

Currently, the necessary condition for the classification of "unemployed" is that, when the census is taken, the individual must have been out of work for a specified minimum of one week. In other words, a worker who happens to be out of work during the census week, even though he is fully employed for the rest of the year, is counted as unemployed. This criterion also overstates the true level of idle labor. Generally speaking, the unemployment category comprises two groups: (1) wageworkers, employers, self-supporting and unpaid family workers who did not work at all during the census week and who were looking for work or waiting to hear the results of work-seeking efforts made within the preceding sixty days; (2) idle laborers who would have been looking for work except that they were temporarily ill, were waiting to report to a new job within thirty days, were waiting to be called back to a job from which they had been laid off, or were convinced that no employment was available in their line of work or in the community. Even with this definition as a guide, it is often difficult to determine who is or is not employed in the totality of persons classified as "unemployed" in the work force (see Gertrude Bancroft, "Current Unemployment Statistics of the Census Bureau and Some Alternatives," in *The Measurement and Behavior of Unemployment*, Conference of the Universities [Princeton: Princeton University Press, 1957], pp. 67–68; Gertrude Deutsche, "How the Unemployed Are Counted," *Business Record* [Dec., 1960], pp. 21–23; Louis J. Ducoff and Margaret J. Hagood, *Labor Force Definition and Measurement: Recent Experience in the United States*, Social Science Research Council, Bulletin no. 56 [New York, 1947]; and W. Galenson and A. Zellner, *International Comparison of Unemployment Rates*, Reprint no. 86, Institute of Industrial Relations, University of California [Berkeley, 1957], pp. 441–446).

but more meaningful term "underemployment"; the meaning of the term will become more clear in chapter iii.

Although the discussion of disguised unemployment has been carried on in economic literature under the assumption of *ceteris paribus,* this term has not been used in a uniform or unequivocal way. Its meaning ranges from the strict interpretation—"everything else being equal"—to the admission of slight changes in methods of organization, and even to a substantial increase in capital. The withdrawal of labor from the land is itself a change which in reality must entail some other change or changes. For example, after some people are withdrawn from the land, the remaining workers may have to do more work to maintain the same amount of total output; and a reshuffling of workers, replacing one person with another, may also occur. In my analysis, however, such limited changes are purposely assumed to be compatible with the *ceteris paribus* assumption. However, the following changes are considered to be incompatible with the assumption: a decrease in total farm output; an increase in capital (monetary or real); the introduction of new technologies, including the adoption of improved seeds or new crops; the diversification of agriculture to compensate for its seasonal nature; and the consolidation of scattered and fragmented landholdings. A change in social institutions is, of course, not compatible with the *ceteris paribus* assumption. Whenever this assumption is relaxed in this study, it is done only for analytical purposes and not in connection with basic assertions and conclusions.

II

The Literature on Disguised Unemployment

The concept of disguised unemployment predominates in current theoretical discussion of the employment problem in underdeveloped countries, but there is little accord among economists writing on this subject. Neither is there unanimity about the nature of employment itself, as a working concept; this concept, as well, has yet to be clearly defined. It is the purpose of this chapter to challenge the validity of several prominent views of disguised unemployment. A critical examination of the meaning of employment will be attempted in a subsequent chapter.

VISIBLE AND INVISIBLE DISGUISED UNEMPLOYMENT

The various approaches to disguised unemployment may be grouped into those dealing with visible types and those dealing with invisible types; these, in turn, may be classified as cyclical, seasonal, and chronic. In reviewing the literature one should perhaps begin with a definition of disguised unemployment put forth by the originator of this concept, Mrs. Joan Robinson:

In a society in which there is no regular system of unemployment benefit, and in which poor relief is either non-existent or "less eligible" than almost any alternative short of suicide, a man who is thrown out of work must scratch up a living somehow or other by means of his own efforts. And under any system in which complete idleness is not a statutory condition for drawing the dole, a man who cannot find a regular job will naturally employ his time as usefully as he may. Thus, except under peculiar conditions, a decline in effective demand which reduces the amount of employment offered in the general run of industries will not lead to "unemployment" in the sense of complete idleness, but will rather drive workers into a number of occupations —selling match-boxes in the Strand, cutting brushwood in the jungles, digging potatoes on allotments—which are still open to them. . . . In all those occupations which the dismissed workers take up, their productivity is less than in the occupations that they have left. . . . The wage received by a man who remains in employment in a particular industry measures the marginal physical productivity of a similar man who has been dismissed from it. . . . The cause of this diversion, a decline in effective demand, is exactly the same as the cause of unemployment in the ordinary sense, and it is natural to describe the adoption of inferior occupations by dismissed workers as *disguised unemployment*. . . . If a revival of investment were to occur, dismissed workers would be called back from the hedgerows and the street-kerbs into their normal occupations. . . . The output of consumption goods, as evaluated by consumers, has therefore increased. Hence, according to our definition, unemployment existed before the revival of investment took place, even though every individual worker was busy all day long.[1]

Mrs. Robinson also maintains that what the dismissed workers produce from their employment in inferior occupations is a clear addition to the total output. When, however, some of these dismissed workers compete with those who have been employed all along in a disguised sense, and when the employment of the former leads to an equivalent curtailment of the employment of the latter, the net addition to the total output of society is zero.[2] The significant element in this line of reasoning is not the marginal productivity of labor employed in the inferior occupations, but rather the differential productivity of labor employed in regular industries and labor employed in inferior occupations. It is this dif-

---

[1] Joan Robinson, *Essays in the Theory of Employment* (2d ed.; Oxford: Basil Blackwell, 1947), pp. 61–62.

[2] *Ibid.*, p. 66.

ference in productivity which supposedly accounts for so-called disguised unemployment.

It should be noted, however, that Mrs. Robinson's distinction between regular and inferior occupations is not clear-cut. Any attempt to classify occupations in underdeveloped economies on the basis of their respective productivities falls into difficulties. Many household goods and services which are objects of exchange in the market place in economically advanced countries are produced by families for their own use in backward societies, and they cannot necessarily be considered inferior. A good example might be the cutting of brushwood for heating and cooking purposes. In densely populated underdeveloped countries firewood is extremely scarce, and therefore very expensive. For unskilled workers, earnings from wage employment would not result in any higher productivity than would the gathering of firewood.

Suppose, for analytical purposes, that household activities are excluded, for the moment, from the discussion, and that only peasant farming and wage employment are considered as regular employment. Then, for one man (A), who has no other employment than cultivation of a plot of land, farming is the regular occupation; for another man (B), who has wage employment in addition to his own farming activity, the wage employment is the regular occupation and farming is the inferior occupation. Now, suppose that both A and B are working on their own farms and that their productivity is the same. As disguised unemployment, according to Mrs. Robinson, connotes inferior employment, B would be considered as being employed in a disguised sense, while A is not. Yet in terms of income, B would be in a better position than A. The absurdity of such theorizing is obvious. Nevertheless, this concept of disguised unemployment has been applied to labor of low productivity employed in a self-supporting status. The Navarretes, for example, attempt to explain Mrs. Robinson's concept of disguised unemployment in three ways: "cyclical (disguised) underemployment," "structural (hidden) underemployment," and "underemployment of expansion." [3]

"Cyclical (disguised) underemployment" is said to result from

[3] Alfredo Navarrete, Jr., and Ifigenia M. de Navarrete, "Underemployment in Underdeveloped Economies," in *The Economics of Underdevelopment,* ed. A. N. Agarwala and S. P. Singh (Bombay: Oxford University Press, 1958), pp. 342–343.

the fluctuation in "foreign demand" for primary products. The extent of "cyclical (disguised) underemployment" is claimed to be a direct function of the importance of foreign trade. The more important the subsistence agricultural sector, the greater the cyclical (disguised) underemployment, as the subsistence agricultural sector serves as shock absorber for the cyclical fluctuation of external demand. It is a well-known fact, however, that the demand for steel and iron is subject to greater cyclical variations than is the demand for primary products in general. Therefore, according to this line of reasoning, even if it is taken for granted that the subsistence sector in economically advanced countries is nonexistent, there may often be much disguised underemployment in such countries whenever a number of workers are laid off. Such workers are said to be underemployed in a disguised sense because they are doing something that is less productive than their former employment. Perhaps they may be engaged in gardening or in repairing furniture.[4] Thus, underemployment due to the cyclical fluctuations of demand is not confined to underdeveloped countries producing primary products. Indeed, this concept of disguised unemployment does not seem to be very helpful as a means of distinguishing unemployment in underdeveloped countries from that in economically advanced countries.

It should also be noted that the price elasticity of most agricultural products is low, so that the volume of output does not change much in the short run, even when the price of the product fluctuates widely. It cannot be said, therefore, that a moderate fall in the demand for primary products would damage employment conditions or create more serious problems than those already existing. In other words, in many underdeveloped agricultural economies, neither physical production nor employment depends on foreign trade in primary products.

Seasonal rather than cyclical unemployment, or underemployment, is the problem of manpower utilization in underdeveloped agricultural countries today. This is true even though labor scarcity in the peak agricultural season is characteristic of these countries. The study made by John Lossing Buck shows that there are labor shortages in almost all of China in the peak agricultural

---

[4] This concept of disguised unemployment would also apply to workers who have gone out on strike or who have been prevented by a strong labor union from being laid off.

season.[5] Transplanting rice seed by hand to the main field is one of the most urgent tasks. It is done in the busiest season of the year, and yet no time must be lost if a good crop is to be obtained. Hoon Koo Lee, in his study of the Korean agricultural problem, states that the lack of improved tools and machines for ploughing, seeding, weeding, and harvesting reduces the efficiency of farm labor and results in too much manual labor for the farmer. Consequently, from early spring to late fall, the farmer has very little leisure time.[6] Even in densely populated areas like Egypt and Java, a labor shortage exists in the periods of peak agricultural labor requirements. In Egypt a large number of child laborers are mobilized for the cultivation of land. In other words, more people are required for more intensive farming methods to help support the increasing population.[7] Louise E. Howard also stresses this point. She feels that "simultaneity" in sowing and harvesting creates a labor shortage. Her description of the difficulties caused by the seasonal nature of agricultural production is most vivid and suggestive:

> Most of the economic and social problems peculiar to agriculture can eventually be traced back to the conditions which we have noted, which are: the unabbreviable interval lying between the effort of sowing and the reward of harvest; the rigid necessity for carrying out operations at the right times; the simultaneous arrival of the harvest for all cultivators together; the irregularity of the amounts reaped contrasted with the insistent demands of living human beings for perfect smoothness of supplies. . . . The problem of maintenance during the "dead" season—the times of inaction and no profits—goes very deep in agriculture. . . . It is a harsh form of organization, but is a form, nevertheless; and it does perform the annual miracle of enabling the peasant to survive and once more to sow his ground as spring comes round.[8]

If the characteristics of agricultural operation are such that the peak requirements of labor are high, so too is the surplus of labor

[5] John Lossing Buck, *Land Utilization in China* (Chicago: University of Chicago Press, 1937), pp. 299–307.

[6] Hoon Koo Lee, *Land Utilization and Rural Economy in Korea* (Chicago: University of Chicago Press, 1936), pp. 96–97.

[7] Doreen Warriner, *Land and Poverty in the Middle East*, Middle East Economic and Social Studies (London: Royal Institute of International Affairs, 1948), p. 103.

[8] Louise E. Howard, *Labour in Agriculture: An International Survey* (London: Oxford University Press, 1935), pp. 8–9.

high in off seasons. The greater the agricultural production in a country, the greater the seasonality of production as a whole, and thus the more serious the problem of seasonal unemployment and underemployment.[9]

"Structural (hidden) underemployment" is, according to the Navarretes, chronic underemployment that is reflected in the willingness of thousands of workers, mostly agricultural, who do not have regular employment during the greater part of the year's normal working period, to work at existing wage rates. Is it not true, however, that this so-called structural (hidden) underemployment is no more than open (and visible) unemployment which arises from the seasonal variations of agricultural operation? It is open in nature because the workers are willing to work at a given wage rate but fail to find employment. Obviously, then, it hardly seems useful to make a special case of open unemployment in underdeveloped countries, as the nature of open unemployment in these economies is basically the same as in economically advanced countries. The position of the Navarretes on this point is no different from saying that disguised underemployment in underdeveloped agricultural countries is the same as open unemployment in economically advanced countries. To claim that hidden (or disguised) unemployment and open unemployment are identical is absurd.

The Navarretes' third type of underemployment—"underemployment of expansion"—is attributed to inadequate economic growth. According to their theory, underemployment results from the failure of capital and other complementary means of production to increase at the same rate as the supply of labor in secondary and tertiary activities. Workers thus find it necessary to engage

---

[9] This, of course, does not apply to countries that have noncereal types of agriculture, and whose lands are not densely populated. For example, in "agricultural factories" like Denmark and New Zealand, the major products are not cereal crops; Denmark imports feed for pigs and exports bacon, doing a sort of finishing process. New Zealand specializes in sheep in a similar manner. This hypothesis also does not apply to some other countries (Switzerland, France, Australia, Canada, and Argentina) where agricultural production is to a marked degree an important activity in the national economy. In Switzerland, dairy products are important. France, which has a more diversified agriculture, produces wine, vegetables, flowers, and fruits. In Australia, meat and dairy products are important, in addition to wheat. And Argentina produces not only wheat but also meat. None of these countries is densely populated, and, in general, none has a problem of surplus labor as such. These countries are, therefore, left out of this discussion.

in activities of very low productivity. They become, for instance, peddlers of all kinds of goods and services requiring little or no capital; they may be vendors of fruit, cigars, lottery tickets, and newspapers, or they may offer their services as bootblacks, porters, waiters, and shop assistants. According to the Navarretes, the magnitude of underemployment of expansion would be in proportion to (rural) hidden underemployment.[10] This type of disguised unemployment—that is, "underemployment of expansion" —is also not unique to underdeveloped countries. The differential of productivity among the three conventional sectors of the economy is substantial in many economically advanced countries.

Another type of invisible disguised unemployment is set forth by Professor Ragnar Nurkse. As his concept differs substantially from the original idea of Mrs. Robinson, and as it is typical of those found in the literature, it deserves to be examined in some detail. According to Nurkse, unemployment in underdeveloped countries is disguised instead of open. The social institutions, particularly the extended family system, do not permit workers to be openly unemployed. This leads to a situation in which many workers merely "appear to be working." Thus, a special artificial kind of full employment prevails; however, this kind of farm labor does not increase total output or even decrease it. Such employment of labor is, from the economic standpoint, no better than no employment at all. And that part of labor which is unemployed in a disguised sense could be withdrawn and put to work on projects supported by "disguised saving" [11] without affecting total output and without substantially changing the method and organization of production.

Nurkse states this contention as follows:

These countries suffer from large-scale disguised unemployment in the sense that, even with unchanged techniques of agriculture, a large part of the population engaged in agriculture could be removed without reducing agricultural output. . . . The term disguised unemployment is not applied to wage labour. It denotes a condition of family employment in peasant communities. A number of people are work-

---

[10] Navarrete and Navarrete, *op. cit.,* p. 343.

[11] "Disguised saving" is, according to Nurkse, the food consumed by those unemployed in a disguised sense (see Ragnar Nurkse, *Problems of Capital Formation in Underdeveloped Countries* [Oxford: Basil Blackwell, 1955], p. 37).

ing on farms or small peasant plots, contributing virtually nothing to output, but subsisting on a share of their family's real income. . . . In technical terms, the marginal productivity of labour, over a wide range, is zero. . . . It is typical of many countries in the area ranging from south-eastern Europe to south-eastern Asia. In these overcrowded peasant economies it is truly a mass phenomenon, due to social, economic and demographic causes.[12]

Unfortunately, almost every point in Nurkse's analysis fails to be congruent with the facts. His assertion that the term "disguised unemployment," or surplus labor, is not applicable to wage labor has no operational validity. Furthermore, he fails to realize or acknowledge that a vast amount of visible idle labor exists. And, finally, he ignores the fact that social institutions, insufficient technical means of production, and congested population are some of the factors that hinder full employment, and that these may be the causes of visible idle labor, rather than the causes of so-called disguised unemployment. All these criticisms will be more fully substantiated later on in this study.

Of immediate concern at this point in the discussion is how Professor Nurkse's concept differs from Mrs. Robinson's. Whereas the latter relates disguised unemployment to the differential productivity between labor in regular industries and labor in inferior occupations, Nurkse's concern is not this differential productivity but only the labor productivity in peasant farming. He clearly states that, even though all workers in agriculture may actually be working, a large number of them may not be contributing to total output, so that the marginal productivity of this kind of working labor is zero. This is clearly a new form of disguised unemployment; and although this new concept vitiates the original one of Mrs. Robinson, it is easier to understand and therefore has become more representative than hers and than those of other economists.

It must be noted, however, that although the general output per capita in these underdeveloped economies is low, this is not necessarily true of the output per labor-hour employed on a given piece of land, as claimed by Nurkse. If the marginal productivity of farm labor employed is low, there are factors besides the insufficiency of technical means of production which explain this

---

[12] *Ibid.*, pp. 32–34.

low level of labor productivity and the impossibility of dispensing
with or withdrawing such labor. These factors include the starvation level of food consumption and the problem of fatigue.
Agricultural work is uniquely fatiguing.

The physical condition of labor in underdeveloped countries
has been emphasized in recent development theory. In terms of
caloric and protein intake, people in these countries consume
roughly 30 to 40 per cent less than those in economically advanced
countries. Underdeveloped countries have a per capita average
daily caloric intake ranging from about 1,900 to 2,500 units; in
economically advanced countries, the intake ranges from about
3,000 to 3,400 units. An implication of Professor Harvey Leibenstein's study is that the people of underdeveloped economies are
not physically able to work so hard as might be expected by those
unfamiliar with their physical condition. Leibenstein concludes
that the people of these countries are fed so poorly that an increase in food consumption would lead to an increase in output
at a relatively higher rate.[13]

In addition to the problem of malnutrition, fatigue presents a
special hardship in peasant farming. Louise Howard's comment
on this factor is applicable to many underdeveloped agricultural
economies:

In any case agricultural work is prone to give an impression of endlessness, just because the processes of Nature are such continuous ones
and never stop; perhaps also because the whole extent of the work is
visible all the time to the worker's eye: placed in the field he gets no
relief from the thought of what is in front of him. This sense of
endlessness is curiously allied with a sense of hurry: however immense
the task, yet it must be mastered with speed if the uncommandable
forces of Nature are not once more to get the upper hand; the natural
factory cannot, in truth, be shut down. All these elements, the element of monotony, the element of endlessness, and the element of
hurry, are powerful contributors to mental fatigue.[14]

After describing the working conditions of the Korean farmer,
Angus Hamilton concludes that "he is content to regard his sphere
of utility in this world as one in which man must labour after

---

[13] Harvey Leibenstein, *Economic Backwardness and Economic Growth: Studies in
the Theory of Economic Development* (New York: John Wiley & Sons, 1960), pp.
62–66.

[14] Howard, *op. cit.*, pp. 233–234.

the fashion of his animals, with no appreciable satisfaction to himself. . . . the farmer of Korea is the ideal child of nature. . . . He is the slave of his work. . . ." [15]

It is not unusual, because of the semistarvation level of food consumption and the element of fatigue, that as many workers as possible are drawn into the fields in order to accomplish the task as quickly as possible. In short, the true picture is not that the farmers merely seem to be working, or that they are unproductively employed in the sense of Nurkse's description, but that the line between work and nonwork or idleness can be clearly drawn. As indicated earlier, the belief that disguised unemployment is a "mass phenomenon" in underdeveloped economies would attribute irrational behavior to the people of these countries. But it is incontrovertible that people of underdeveloped countries are not any more prone to working without expected rewards than are people in economically advanced countries, although the nature of the rewards may differ. Although it is true that, as the size of the family increases, the number of hours of work per worker tends to decrease, it is unquestionable that when one is actually working he is not wasting his time and labor; he is productive.

The farm worker's poor physical condition, which may be due to inadequate food consumption and the fatiguing nature of agricultural labor, must be taken into full account in determining the reasons for the marginal productivity of such labor. If these factors of malnutrition and fatigue are considered, one could even make a case for hidden employment rather than for disguised (hidden) unemployment, in the sense that an undernourished man doing exhausting work may be overworking. Thus farm labor that may seem to be withdrawable from the land is not actually surplus labor under the constraint of the *ceteris paribus* assumption.

Despite the fact that there has been so much difficulty in accepting the various concepts of disguised unemployment, John Lossing Buck's data on Chinese agriculture have often been cited as proof of the existence of disguised unemployment. Buck writes:

Evidently as the size of farm increases, as measured by crop hectares, the man-work units per man-equivalent do not increase at the same rate. This may be caused by a smaller amount of work being done

---

[15] Angus Hamilton, *Korea* (Boston and Tokyo: J. B. Millet Co., 1910), pp. 56–57.

per hectare on the larger farms, thus keeping the man-work units from increasing in the same proportion. A difference in the amount of work for the same crop, or for different crops, affects such a relationship.[16]

Buck's point here is that on smaller farms more than proportionate human (and animal) labor is used, as compared with larger farms, to produce approximately the same average crop per unit of land. (He does not impute the same to total farm receipts.) "Buck's data do not suffice to show," Professor Jacob Viner comments, "that the marginal productivity of labor was less on the smaller farms than on the larger ones, and certainly do not suffice to show that there is zero marginal productivity of labor anywhere in the Chinese economy." [17]

Buck's data are not detailed enough to show the productivity of employed labor. His study, based on "man-equivalent" statistics (man-equivalent signifying one man working on the farm for twelve months), does not show the precise amount of labor employed on the farm. More useful data could be obtained by investigating man-hour equivalents, not man-equivalents, because in such an economy the line between time devoted to farm activities and nonfarm activities is difficult to draw. In an economy where workers are not continuously working and where the degree of division of labor is relatively low, the productivity of labor, measured in terms of persons, is very misleading. Furthermore, Buck's study, based on crop yields per acre, does not show the over-all productivity of workers. In this context it is the total farm output or total farm receipts (i.e., crop and noncrop receipts) per unit of land, not the crop yields per unit of land, which are relevant to the productivity of labor. The crop yield per hectare is about the same on farms of different sizes, but the total farm output per hectare is not. In fact, Buck's own data show that total farm receipts per hectare on smaller farms were much higher than on larger farms. On small farms (.96 hectares) the farm receipts per hectare averaged $221.26; on medium-sized farms (2.47 hectares), $196.58; and on large farms (5.66 hectares), $171.66.[18]

---

[16] John Lossing Buck, *Chinese Farm Economy* (Chicago: University of Chicago Press, 1930), p. 130.

[17] Jacob Viner, "Some Reflections on the Concept of 'Disguised Unemployment,'" *Indian Journal of Economics*, XXXVIII (July, 1957), 20.

[18] Buck, *Chinese Farm Economy*, table 18, p. 448.

There are other factors that challenge the traditional interpretation of Buck's empirical data. They show that land values per hectare of smaller farms are greater than those of larger farms.[19] This evidence implies that more labor has been applied to the improvement of the land on small farms than on large farms. But the larger farms may have been originally more fertile and better located (e.g., with better access to water sources). It may also be that the farmers of small holdings are physically weaker than those with larger landholdings. In any event, the contention that the farmers of small holdings apply more labor than those of large holdings, without increasing output, is not warranted.

Perhaps the most notable contribution to the clarification of some of the problems of employment in underdeveloped agricultural countries has been made by Hsieh Chiang.[20] According to Chiang, there are three different ways in which it may be possible to withdraw labor without affecting agricultural output: (1) It may be possible to withdraw a certain amount of agricultural labor without changing the method of production and without reducing agricultural output. This withdrawn labor constitutes "visible unemployment." (2) A further amount of labor could be released from the farm by introducing simple and already known laborsaving changes in the method of agricultural production which require little or no additional capital. It may be possible, for example, to raise the intensity of work and to increase the division of labor, to introduce simple laborsaving devices requiring little or no net addition to capital expenditure, and to change land tenure arrangements. (3) Additional labor could be released without affecting agricultural output by introducing more fundamental changes in the method of production (and also perhaps in its organization) which require substantial capital investment. In this situation there exists, in Chiang's terminology, "potential underemployment." [21]

According to Chiang, the above three types of nonemployment conditions are chronic, in the sense that even at the peak of agricultural activity the potential amount of labor time still exceeds

[19] *Ibid.*

[20] Hsieh Chiang, "Underemployment in Asia. I. Nature and Extent," *International Labour Review*, LXV (June, 1952), 703–725.

[21] *Ibid.*, pp. 710–711.

the amount of labor time actually utilized.[22] Visible unemployment, however, does involve both seasonal and chronic unemployment. Visible seasonal and chronic unemployment do not, according to Chiang, constitute disguised unemployment, because those thus affected are not working. According to him, insofar as only visible chronic unemployment exists, there is no problem of releasing surplus labor. However, Chiang's treatment of visible chronic unemployment as withdrawable surplus labor, under the *ceteris paribus* assumption, is questionable, because not all visible chronic unemployment is involuntary. Voluntary chronic unemployment is not available for withdrawal under the *ceteris paribus* assumption. The belief that all the visible chronic unemployment can be released from the land fails to take into account underlying motives for being or remaining thus unemployed.

Chiang's "disguised underemployment" (instead of "disguised unemployment") is also misleading. He has two different meanings for "underemployment," but he says nothing about the meaning of the term "disguised" itself. He defines "underemployment" as the condition of a laborer who works less than the standard number of hours, and at the same time, as workers with a low level of productivity.[23] His first concept of underemployment conforms with what is here termed "visible partial unemployment," whereas the condition that is described in the second definition is not visible, as the laborer is actually employed in economic operation though with a low level of productivity.

It is relevant here to note Rosenstein-Rodan's concept of disguised unemployment. In his study on Italy he defines "disguised underemployment" as that amount of idle work force, in terms of man-equivalent hours, which exists at the peak of the agricultural operation.[24] (This disguised underemployment is exactly the same as Chiang's visible chronic unemployment.) Rosenstein-Rodan divides disguised underemployment into "removable" and "fractional" underemployment. "Removable disguised underem-

---

[22] *Ibid.*, p. 708.
[23] *Ibid.*, pp. 704, 709.
[24] P. N. Rosenstein-Rodan, "Disguised Unemployment and Underemployment in Agriculture," *Monthly Bulletin of Agricultural Economics and Statistics,* VI (July-Aug., 1957), 7.

ployment" (equivalent to his concept of disguised unemployment) comprises those workers who are employed very little during the year, that is, for less than fifty-one days per year (or less than two calendar months).[25] The removal of these workers is thought not to cause agricultural output to decline and not to change the agricultural organization, except that hired workers would be substituted for them for less than fifty-one days per year, the tolerable minimum change compatible with the *ceteris paribus* assumption. "Fractional disguised underemployment" comprises those workers who are partially employed (for more than 51 days) during the year. These workers, according to Rosenstein-Rodan, are not "removable disguised underemployment" because their removal would mean a substantial violation of the *ceteris paribus* assumption.

Rosenstein-Rodan's study evokes several comments. First, those who he claims are underemployed in a "disguised" sense are essentially "visible" chronic idle labor. It hardly seems meaningful to identify visible with disguised unemployment. Second, Rosenstein-Rodan's claim that only "removable disguised underemployment" is surplus or excess labor underestimates the true level of surplus labor. The "fractional disguised underemployment" that could be mobilized for economic development projects in and near the villages is also essentially surplus labor.

Still another concept of disguised unemployment is that of Harvey Leibenstein, who believes it is caused mainly by the seasonal fluctuation of agricultural operations. He states that

. . . subtraction of a portion of the labor force will yield a smaller output no matter what sort of reorganization of the smaller labor force takes place. Similarly, an addition to the labor force would result in a higher total yield. The sense in which we can have disguised unemployment in this case is that with additional resources or means of creating additional employment opportunities *of the right kind, more effort* could be obtained from the existing labor force. This type of unemployment is due to the seasonal nature of the production process in agriculture, coupled with the fact that there is a lack of alternative employment outlets. . . . The agricultural labor force may be said to suffer from disguised unemployment in the same

---

[25] *Ibid.*, p. 5.

sense that taxi-drivers may be said to suffer from disguised unemployment.[26]

Leibenstein's "disguised unemployment" is similar to Chiang's "visible seasonal unemployment." Chiang is correct in his statement that visible seasonal unemployment is not disguised unemployment.

One may find a vast amount of disguised unemployment, in Leibenstein's sense of the term, even in economically well-advanced countries. Not only taxi drivers, but all those whose labor is not continuously applied, fall into the category of disguised unemployment, according to Leibenstein. Furthermore, the concept of disguised unemployment by and large precludes a substantial change in method or organization. Excessive violation of this (*ceteris paribus*) assumption leads nowhere but to so-called potential unemployment.[27] The contention here is that the identification of either chronic or seasonal visible unemployment with disguised unemployment hardly seems logical.

The preceding analysis particularly emphasizes one point: the concept of disguised unemployment based on labor productivity, either of labor employed or of labor not employed, is inadequate to explain the problem of manpower utilization in underdeveloped agricultural economies, and thus does not help to determine the possible volume of surplus labor.

WAGE LABOR VERSUS SELF-SUPPORTING FAMILY LABOR

The traditional treatment of the subject of wage labor and self-supporting family labor also confuses the issue, and is misleading in any attempt to estimate the amount of withdrawable surplus labor. A United Nations group states: "The significance of the term 'disguised' is that it is applied only to persons who are not normally engaged in wage employment. The disguised unemployed are those persons who work on their own account. . . . The term is not applied to wage labour; presumably employers

---

[26] Leibenstein, *op. cit.*, p. 60.
[27] Chiang, *op. cit.*, pp. 710–711.

will not employ a labourer for wages unless his labour increases the total product." [28] The term "normally" in the above quotation suggests that a wage laborer is one who works for wages more than one-half of his working time, or for more than one-half of his income. In estimating disguised unemployment or surplus labor, one cannot help but wonder whether wage labor should be included or excluded. If one follows the United Nations criterion cited above, wage laborers must be excluded from disguised unemployment. In some countries, however, wage labor is a very large proportion of the agricultural work force, so that the more-than-one-half criterion will seriously underestimate the volume of surplus labor.

The Agricultural Labour Enquiry, conducted by the Indian government in 1951, adopted the more-than-one-half criterion. It found that, for India as a whole, about 32 per cent of the total agricultural earners, or about 35 million workers, were wage laborers.[29] That is too large a number to be excluded from the estimate of disguised unemployment; but it is, paradoxically, also too large a number to be included, because such inclusion would destroy the meaning of "disguised" unemployment. In fact, the orthodox concept holds that, if the proportion of wage labor to self-supporting family labor (on the basis of the one-half criterion) increases with all other things being kept unchanged, the magnitude of disguised unemployment must decrease and could reach a point where one could see no surplus labor at all, although the people remained as poor as before. This absurd criterion owes its existence to the excessive adherence to the yardstick of the productivity of labor employed. It is difficult to understand, therefore, what significance the one-half criterion can have for the measurement of disguised unemployment.

Nevertheless, the position taken by the United Nations group

---

[28] United Nations, Department of Economic Affairs, *Measures for the Economic Development of Under-developed Countries* (New York, 1951), p. 7.

[29] India, Ministry of Labour, *Agricultural Labour Enquiry: Report on Intensive Survey of Agricultural Labour*, I (Delhi, 1955), 37–44; Daniel and Alice Thorner, "Agricultural Manpower in India: Labourers," *Economic Weekly*, IX (Nov., 1957), 1443–1449; Reserve Bank Rural Credit Survey Team, "Surplus Labour in Agriculture: Has It Been Sized Up?" *Economic Weekly*, VII (Aug., 1955), 954; "Agricultural Labour. I. Pattern of Occupation and Employment," *Economic Weekly*, VII (Aug., 1955), 937–939; and Daniel Thorner, "The Agricultural Labour Enquiry: Reflections on Concepts and Methods," *Economic Weekly*, XIII (June, 1956), 758–766.

on the concept of nonzero productivity of wage labor has led certain economists to assume that the term "diguised unemployment" does not apply to wage labor.[30] But the evidence of a substantial amount of labor exchange outside the labor market further blurs the concept. This exchange of family labor is one of the important features of the so-called village economy that still prevails in Asia.[31] Although such supply and demand for family labor through labor coöperation does not appear directly in the market, it certainly will reduce the number of agricultural wage laborers. As mutual labor coöperation occurs mainly in the busy seasons, one cannot assume that any unnecessary exchange of labor (unnecessary in the sense that its marginal productivity is zero) would occur. Specifically, family workers need not be employed in a disguised sense on the basis of a one-day, one-week, or one-month period when they help others. For this reason the question again arises as to whether this part of family labor should or should not be excluded from the estimate of disguised unemployment. On the basis of the marginal productivity criterion, this part of family labor must be excluded, but it cannot be excluded on the basis of the United Nations more-than-one-half criterion.

THE ROLE OF SOCIAL INSTITUTIONS IN EMPLOYMENT

What role do social institutions play in connection with employment conditions in these underdeveloped economies? Do they really cause so unnecessary an application of labor as to leave labor with a zero marginal productivity, or, rather, could they be a cause of visible idle labor? These are most important questions in connection with the concept of disguised unemployment. In short, the role of social institutions in so-called disguised unemployment seems to have been largely misinterpreted by the orthodox school of thought on this subject. The following passage gives a clearer insight into Mrs. Robinson's concept: "If a dole

---

[30] Nurkse, *op. cit.*, p. 33; Gerald M. Meier and Robert E. Baldwin, *Economic Development: Theory, History, Policy* (New York: John Wiley & Sons, 1957), p. 282.

[31] "Village economy" refers to a type of community farming that was characteristic of the European medieval period and is still prevalent today, though in a somewhat different form, in the family farming of many underdeveloped countries.

is instituted, for which complete idleness is a qualification, the result will be an increase of employment and output in regular industries, combined with a decrease of disguised unemployment. It will cause unemployment to throw off the disguise, but, from the point of view of regular industry, the amount of unemployment will be reduced." [32]

Mrs. Robinson's concept of disguised unemployment can, perhaps, be even better elucidated if one thinks of a society where there is no dole system of any kind. In such a society, there is neither any kind of government relief payment nor any traditional social institutions that would provide relief, such as a share of the total family income. Given these conditions, the dismissed workers from "regular industries" must "scratch up a living" by employing themselves in "inferior occupations." The dole to which Mrs. Robinson refers is apparently not the same as the unique social function performed by such traditional institutions as the extended family, caste, or clan system. These social institutions in reality serve a function very similar to regular relief payment, through the sharing of output with all members of the extended family. In short, in many underdeveloped agricultural communities, there is a "dole" system. Its existence (although complete idleness for a long period of time is, of course, not a customary condition for drawing it) is more likely to cause visible underemployment than disguised unemployment. This point is important because later writers on this subject have almost all taken the opposite position, that disguised unemployment (of employed labor) is caused by traditional social institutions.

This view, that traditional social institutions are the cause of disguised unemployment, is almost unconditionally accepted. Professor Nurkse, among others, believes that in a society where the extended family system is an accepted way of life, disguised unemployment, as he defines it, is inevitable; and such labor, with a marginal productivity of zero, will become surplus with the given changes in organization.[33] According to Nurkse, in the area

---

[32] Robinson, *op. cit.*, pp. 68–69.

[33] Nurkse, *op. cit.*, p. 32. See also W. A. Lewis, "Economic Development with Unlimited Supplies of Labour," *Manchester School of Economic and Social Studies,* XXII (May, 1954), 142; and Berdj Kenadjian, "Disguised Unemployment in Underdeveloped Countries" (unpublished Ph.D. thesis, Harvard University, 1957), pp. 95–96.

ranging from southeastern Europe to southeastern Asia, such surplus labor may constitute from 15 to 50 per cent of the entire labor force.[34]

Even those who question the concept of disguised unemployment do not seem to have understood the role of social institutions as interpreted by Mrs. Robinson. K. N. Raj and Jacob Viner are examples. According to Raj, the zero marginal productivity of labor employed (and labor not actually employed, i.e., idle labor) is due entirely to the traditional social organization, and such labor with zero marginal productivity becomes "manpower surplus" with given assumed changes in organization. Raj writes:

Now, it is obvious that the rates of capital formation, technical change, and population growth are intimately connected with the problem of unemployment, and more so with the level of productivity and real income at which employment opportunities are open. . . . But to define employment and unemployment in terms of productivity of labour for this reason would be to mix what is primarily a social phenomenon with a technical fact which, however pertinent to its solution, is not uniquely correlated with it. Labour with a marginal productivity of zero will be part of manpower surplus, which can become available with given assumed changes in organization, but it will not be treated as part of the currently unemployed if the existing social organization permits them to be idle or disguises the fact that they contribute nothing in reality to the social output, despite their appearing to do so.[35]

Raj's attempt to relate the problem of manpower utilization in these economies entirely to the social organization adds further confusion. He overlooks the fact, although it seems quite obvious, that regardless of the different types of social organization there exists visible idle labor owing to technical and institutional conditions inherent in the economy. The inelasticity of production, and the seasonal variation of agricultural production, are, given the *ceteris paribus* assumption, beyond the control of those whom the social organization permits to be idle. The seasonal law does not discriminate among different types of social organization.

---

[34] Nurkse, *op. cit.*, p. 35.

[35] K. N. Raj, *Employment Aspects of Planning in Underdeveloped Economies*, National Bank of Egypt, Fiftieth Anniversary Commemoration Lecture (Cairo, 1957), pp. 4–5.

The point here, of course, is that one must distinguish, when possible, between labor idle as a result of the traditional value system and labor that is idle because of nontraditional factors.

Even Professor Viner, who has criticized the impreciseness and the ambiguity surrounding the concept of disguised unemployment, does not seem to have grasped this point. He believes that "non-economic motivation" could be a cause of hiring wage labor "beyond the point at which they [employers] know that labor will not add to, or may even subtract from, the product." [36] He fails to see that noneconomic motivation has meaning only in a limited sense, even in an economically poor society. Specifically, even if one assumes noneconomic motivation on the part of employers, the marginal productivity of wage labor could not be zero; for, as the real income of farm owners (i.e., employers) as a whole is also very minimal, there is no real likelihood of hiring so many units of wage labor as to create labor with a zero marginal productivity. In these economically poor societies the function of the noneconomic value system is very much constrained by individual economic conditions, and, likewise, the function of the economic value system is constrained by noneconomic causes. This is to say that both economic and noneconomic factors are equally important in the total value system of these societies.

CONCLUSION

In underdeveloped countries today visible underemployment, instead of disguised unemployment, constitutes a basic characteristic of employment conditions. To say that the employed are unemployed in disguise is to say that people in these countries are so irrational as to use labor unnecessarily. It is, of course, accurate to say that social institutions in these societies are important determinants of the range of choice and the decisions made, but it is not accurate to assert that adjustment to the social institutions is irrational.

The concept of disguised unemployment in general confuses the issue of surplus labor and is not acceptable as a working con-

---

[36] Viner, *op. cit.,* p. 18.

cept of employment and unemployment. As Professor Viner states, its meaning is imprecise and ambiguous. We must find a clearer and more usable criterion for the problem of manpower utilization in underdeveloped agricultural economies. Unless we do this, we shall not be able to understand the real significance of the problem or to adopt proper policies. Let us turn, therefore, to an alternative approach.

III

An Alternative Theoretical Model of Manpower Utilization

Technical and Tradition-directed Underemployment

In chapter ii I pointed out the principal weaknesses of the concept of disguised unemployment: (1) the confusing multiplicity of different conceptions of disguised unemployment—visible and invisible disguised unemployment, underemployment as disguised unemployment, disguised underemployment, and other variations; (2) the vagueness of productivity criteria upon which some of the concepts are based; (3) the failure to distinguish between wage labor and self-supporting family labor in relation to disguised unemployment; (4) the misunderstanding of the role of the "dole" system in tradition-directed societies; and (5) the distortion of the *ceteris paribus* assumption, which invalidates much of the meaning and nature of so-called disguised unemployment and exaggerates the existing amount of true surplus labor.

In order to find an alternative approach to the problem of manpower utilization in underdeveloped agricultural economies, the following steps will be taken: (1) We will use the concept of marginal individuals and its relation to the concept of surplus labor. (2) We will discuss the apparent differences in the systems of employment in two contrasting societies—one with, and another without, traditional social institutions. It will be shown as an analytical model that, in a community where strong institutional values exist, open unemployment is not prevalent, for the presumably "unemployed," who, it may be assumed, have no place to go, are absorbed into farm households and the total work available is shared among the entire work force. In other words, underemployment is truly prevalent. In the course of analysis it will be shown that the marginal productivity of labor actually working, regardless of type of social organization, cannot be zero. (3) We will also discuss the meaning of surplus labor; underemployment will be classified into the technical and tradition-directed varieties, and only technical underemployment will be regarded as removable (or true) surplus labor.

BASIC POSTULATES: THE RELATIONSHIP BETWEEN MARGINAL INDIVIDUALS AND SURPLUS LABOR

The marginal individual,[1] as conceived in this study, is one who is poised in uncertainty between two (or more) apparently different social worlds. The individual who leaves one social or economic group without making a satisfactory "adjustment" to enter another, finds himself on the margin of each but a member of neither. In this sense he is a marginal individual. Because of his uncertain position, from a social or an economic standpoint, he is particularly likely to try to make new adjustments in situations of change. For example, a self-supporting family worker living in a society where tradition and custom dictate the course of his destiny is well adjusted to this reasonably stable and organized society, and is hardly susceptible to removal from his social world. He is not socially a marginal individual. On the other hand, a man who has left self-supporting family farming to make a new life for himself in the city may not be satisfactorily adjusted to

---

[1] For a discussion of the concept of the "marginal individual" see, for example, Everett V. Stonequist, *The Marginal Man: A Study in Personality and Culture Conflict* (New York: Charles Scribner's Sons, 1937), pp. 1–9; Robert E. Park, *Race and Culture* (Chicago: Free Press of Glencoe, 1950), pp. 345–392; and Berthold F. Hoselitz, *Sociological Aspects of Economic Growth* (New York: Free Press of Glencoe, 1960), pp. 66–67.

the new environment, as an unspecified or vague "homesickness," or nostalgia for his previous village life, still lingers. Because of his uncertain attitude toward his current social position, he could easily be taken out of this new environment. In this sense he is socially a marginal individual.

Apart from the cultural point of view, some people engaged in (poor) peasant farming may be regarded as economically marginal individuals, for they may be poised in ambivalence between the desire for a higher material scale of living in some distant industrial area and the material conditions of the life they know. In the presence of this apparent conflict, these people are especially likely to make new adjustments whenever a change in the economic structure occurs.

It is assumed in this study that only those who are both socially and economically marginal could be considered as withdrawable surplus labor. In their minds the elements of choice come together and exist in conflict for a time; eventually such individuals arrive at a judgment, and make the decision to change. Those who are not socially, but only economically, marginal are not regarded as withdrawable surplus labor; they could, however, be mobilized for economic development projects near their villages. They could be removed permanently from their social environment only as a result of a drastic social change, for they would not be particularly suited to making new adjustments in situations of minor change. Those who are socially marginal but economically not marginal are not considered as surplus labor; the likelihood of finding people in such a category in a typical impoverished, underdeveloped rural area is small indeed.

QUALIFIED DEFINITIONS OF "FLOOR" WAGE AND "CEILING" WAGE

Wage structures are usually discussed in terms of two limits—a "floor" and a "ceiling." There is, however, no universal agreement as to their definition or meaning.[2] In this study the "floor"

---

[2] W. A. Lewis, "Economic Development with Unlimited Supplies of Labour," *Manchester School of Economic and Social Studies*, XXII (May, 1954), 148–151.

is defined as a biological minimum to sustain an employed worker
or to keep him alive; and the "ceiling" is defined as a wage that
is adequate not only for biological necessity but also for the maintenance of the worker's status in a given social environment.
Some, however, may regard a wage that simply meets their biological needs as a minimum wage, whereas for others the minimum
wage may be a sociobiological minimum in the sense of the classical dictum that the requirements for a minimum scale of living in
a society may vary, not simply through biological necessity, but
also because of desired social status. Thus, either the floor or the
ceiling could be merely a subsistence wage, in spite of the fact
that the wage rates may differ.

Biologically, an average man needs a minimum of about 1,700
calories a day to keep himself alive. A man carrying earth in a
basket from a canal bottom, however, needs an additional 150
calories per hour, or an extra food requirement of 1,200 calories
in eight hours.[3] The subsistence (the floor) wage is, then, something that just enables employed workers (not jobless workers) to
live. If 2,900 calories are required to sustain a man doing a given
task for eight hours a day, then the biological floor is 2,900
calories.

In this study, which deals with underdeveloped countries, consumption is rigidly held to be the goal of economic activity. In
economically advanced countries, an increase in consumption may
be desirable for its own sake.[4] In underdeveloped countries, however, a rise in consumption is desirable not only for its own sake,
but also because it will lead to an increase in labor effort. Because of this direct relationship between consumption and labor

---

The wage in the "capitalist sector," to which Lewis refers, is a kind of "ceiling."
See also K. N. Raj, *Employment Aspects of Planning in Underdeveloped Economies*,
National Bank of Egypt, Fiftieth Anniversary Commemoration Lecture (Cairo,
1957), p. 10. According to Lewis, the floor corresponds to a wage level (per man)
in the subsistent agricultural sector, whereas the ceiling corresponds to a wage that
prevails in the "capitalistic sector" for homogeneous workers. Raj classifies wages
similarly.

[3] N. Koestner, "Some Comments on Professor Nurkse's Capital Accumulation in
Underdeveloped Countries," *L'Egypte Contemporaine*, XLIV (April, 1953), 9.

[4] Harvey Leibenstein, *Economic Backwardness and Economic Growth: Studies in
the Theory of Economic Development* (New York: John Wiley & Sons, 1960), pp.
63–65; Dipak Mazumdar, "The Marginal Productivity Theory of Wages and
Disguised Unemployment," *Review of Economic Studies*, XXVI (June, 1959), 190–
197; and Paul Wonnacott, "Disguised and Overt Unemployment in Underdeveloped
Countries," *Quarterly Journal of Economics*, LXXVI (May, 1962), 279–297.

effort, it would be in the economic interest of the community to prevent the subsistence consumption from falling. It is, therefore, possible to assume a floor below which no wages would sink if production is to be carried out by the workers. This (biological) wage minimum can be seen as a technical minimum in a given economy. We shall call this minimum a "technical wage."

The social considerations in determining whether or not a given wage is a minimum are of even greater subtlety and importance in underdeveloped countries than in other societies. In underdeveloped countries, traditional social institutions are rigid and must be viewed as an unquestionably integral part of the total value system. Social institutions such as the village, the clan, and the extended-family system exert significant influence on the system of employment. A system of employment made up of self-supporting family farming would be quite different from another system made up largely of wage employment.

The traditional social organization represents special values for those who live within it. Farm-owning family members find a sense of security with regard to their need for labor by having their close relatives in their households. In the face of an ever-repeating crop cycle, continuity in the availability of labor provides a hedge against a labor shortage in peak agricultural seasons. Nonfarm-owning family members, on the other hand, find employment security through their family ties with farm-owning family members. Above all, strong family, clan, and village ties give both farm-owning and nonfarm-owning family members a sense of "belonging," mutual trust, a nondisciplined life, and peace of mind. (Some agricultural economists have even claimed that family farming promotes a team spirit that results in increased efficiency of labor.)

It should be noted, though, that these benefits are not without their own cost. Landless workers do not drift away from the land; consequently, the total work available, and the resulting joint product, are shared among all members of the family. It is this system of employment that constitutes virtually a system of underemployment; unemployment in the usual sense is not possible under this social system. In this traditional society, savings are small or nonexistent, and there is very little labor mobility. The possibility of new adjustments in situations of minor change is remote. Individuals are not socially marginal, and therefore are not surplus labor in the sense that they can be removed from the land permanently.

The possible degree of underemployment, and the sharing of the resulting joint product, will, given the technical means of production, depend on the number of family workers. It goes almost without saying that the degree of underemployment in a "poor" agricultural community is very high, and that as a result the average level of consumption is very low.

Now let us assume a hypothetical situation in which the traditional social organization has been completely broken down. We are conjecturing, in other words, a sudden and far-reaching change in the social institutions. Such a change will hereafter be referred to as a basically different social arrangement or social change. It should be pointed out, in passing, that we are here still dealing with a "poor" underdeveloped economy, even though we have relaxed the *ceteris paribus* assumption and are allowing hypothetical social changes only for the sake of this specific analysis. The breakdown of the social organization would immediately eliminate the system of self-supporting extended-family farming. This would uproot and leave openly unemployed a number of formerly underemployed workers who would have to seek work elsewhere or remain in the same village in a state of chronic unemployment. This would result in more employment for the remaining employed workers. For the uprooted worker (who would now be a potential wageworker), the old dole system—that is, an automatic share in the family output—would no longer be available. He would, when employed, be paid on the basis of marginal productivity.

An alternative to self-supporting family farming, in our hypothetical situation of social change, would be this system of employment made up mostly of wageworkers. The choice between self-supporting family farming and wage employment would be governed by the comparison between the values attributed to the social institutions on the one hand, and the negative values attributed to the system of wage employment on the other. Workers would not give up family farming unless the alternative (wage employment) brought sufficient additional remuneration to offset the advantages of the prevailing system. If such remuneration was superior to what they would have to give up, self-supporting family labor would shift from family farming to wage employment. Conversely, those who are employed for wages would give up this employment and return to the family farm where a certain minimum scale of living is available to them, if the remuneration from wages was no better than what they would have earned had they remained on the farm. Thus, it is possible to assume a ceiling wage that would compensate for the various values attached to family farming over and above the technical (or biological) wage.

The ceiling wage, therefore, may be seen as a sociobiological minimum to self-supporting family workers. Consequently, there is a distinct difference between the biological minimum and the sociobiological minimum. A self-supporting family worker who recognizes this gap is not a socially marginal individual and is not surplus labor in the sense that he could be withdrawn permanently from his social environment.

In the next two sections of this chapter we shall still be discussing the hypothetical situation of the breakdown of the extended-family system of production, that is, a basic social reorganization resulting in a system of much more extensive wage employment.

THE SYSTEM OF EMPLOYMENT IN A "CAPITALISTIC" SOCIETY

To simplify the analysis, we shall assume that (1) workers are homogeneous, are economically equally situated, and have no dependents; and, in order to set apart the intrinsic nature of an underdeveloped country from that of other countries, that (2) the productivity of labor in underdeveloped agricultural economies is not independent of the level of real earnings (or the consumption level), and, finally, that (3) there are no seasonal variations in the demand for labor.

The vertical axis in figure 1 measures the wage rate; the horizontal axis to the right of O, the labor-hour rate. The wage rate may be postulated as the daily caloric intake by a workingman (e.g., 2,500 calories per man per day). A labor-hour refers to the effective physical and mental exertion of labor. For example, a labor-hour in this sense might mean either (1) that if one consumed a hearty breakfast, lunch, and dinner, he would be able to plow a whole acre of given land with the aid of given tools and animals during an eight-hour workday, whereas, if he was poorly fed, he would be able to plow only half an acre; or (2) that one would be able to work the full eight hours during the day if he ate good meals, whereas, if his consumption was poor, his work hours would be cut to perhaps half the ordinary workday.

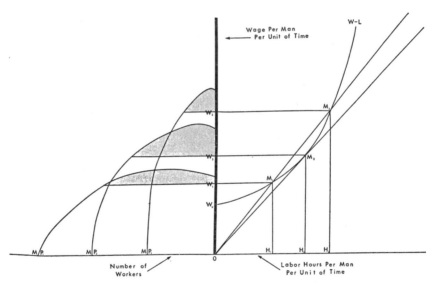

Fig. 1. Wage-productivity relationship of wage labor.

The latter implies that the working hours are cut short because of quick physical fatigue; the former implies employment all day long at a low intensity of work. In many underdeveloped agricultural economies the first situation is possible, but the second is more likely to obtain. As pointed out in the preceding chapter, the characteristics of farm work (fatigue and monotony) are such that it seems more reasonable to expect a shorter workday than a longer workday with low intensity of work. The point is that once we admit the possibility of a functional relationship between labor effort and the level of consumption, the effect of poor consumption on labor effort seems manifest more in the form of shorter hours of work performed than in the low intensity of work with a longer workday.

Thus, the wage–labor-hour relationship may be reduced to the simple concept that the man-hours employed may vary with the wage rates paid to the worker. Despite the fact that the relationship between consumption and labor effort may be much more complex, the concept of labor effort observed and interpreted in this manner is easy to comprehend and readily applicable to the estimate of surplus labor.

The W-L (wage-labor) curve shows the relationship between the wage rate and the labor-hour rate of wageworkers; it deals only with the biological minimum wage. At the earning rate of OW_0, no labor-hours can be supplied, as OW_0 is the rock-bottom biological minimum for keeping a man barely alive (about 1,700 calories a day). Actually, he cannot work at all at this very low level of consumption. Therefore, if a wage rate is to be workable, in the sense of ensuring labor performed, it must be above this level. We shall call this minimum of OW_0 a life-subsistence consumption minimum.

But the observation that people do actually work implies that they must be receiving a wage higher than OW_0. In fact, from the assumptions that have been made, the amount of work done bears a fixed relationship to the wage rate, and consumption must be above OW_0 before any labor-hours are available. For example, at the earning rate of OW_1, OH_1 labor-hours are supplied per man; likewise, OH_2 labor-hours are supplied by a wageworker when the earning rate becomes OW_2. The curve rises slowly at first, then rapidly, showing that, as the earning rate rises, the labor-hours per man increase rapidly, and then slowly. The point M_2 on the W-L curve gives the point at which the wage per labor-hour is the lowest. Thus M_2 is the point on W-L which is just tangent to a straight line drawn through the origin. It is clear that any other line through the origin which lies above OM_2 must cut the W-L curve twice. For this reason, either OH_1 or OH_3 labor-hours are supplied by a worker for the same wage per labor-hour (i.e., $OW_1/OH_1 = OW_3/OH_3$).

Once we admit the possibility that the labor-hours vary with the wage received, the wage rates are in fact a series of technical

wages. Starting from, let us say, 1,850 calories per man per day
(a wage rate just above the life-subsistence level, which enables a
man to start working), the W-L curve indicates a series of technical wages that enable the worker to exert more labor; and this
is the supply curve of labor in terms of labor-hours under a capitalistic agrarian social arrangement, hypothetically introduced into
an erstwhile tradition-directed, extended-family system.

Let us now consider determinants of the wage rate. Under this
impersonal employer-employee arrangement, employers try to
maximize profit by means of extracting maximum labor effort per
dollar as long as it is possible and profitable to do so. Consequently, the wage rate should never be expected to settle below
OW_2, which represents the minimum wage per labor-hour in
terms of wages per laborer.[5] The existence of large numbers of
unemployed workers cannot depress the wage rate below OW_2
because it already is the minimum wage per labor-hour obtainable
and therefore represents the profit-maximizing wage.

From the employer's standpoint, hired workers are as "fully
employed" as possible. If the work force is made up of family
labor instead of wage labor, this "full employment" situation
would not prevail, as explained in the following section. In this
"poor" economy, the competitive wage can no longer be determined by the intersection of supply and demand curves for labor,
because the supply curve itself changes with the wage levels.[6]

In this hypothetical impersonal society, employers would not
be concerned in any way with the problems of the openly unemployed. This point will be understood more clearly if the relationship between the wage rate and the labor-hour rate is expressed in terms of the wageworker relationship, as in Leibenstein's model.[7]

The horizontal axis on the left side in figure 1 measures the
number of workers. The position and the slope of the marginal-
product curve will now be explained briefly. There is a series of
marginal-product (MP) curves of workers, reflecting a series of dif-

---

[5] As OW_2 represents the laborer's take-home pay, any additional costs directly
associated with the size of an employer's work force, and classifiable as labor costs,
will tend to raise the *per laborer* wage rate above OW_2 as substitution takes place.

[6] Mazumdar, *op. cit.*, p. 190, has made this point clear.

[7] Leibenstein, *op. cit.*, pp. 63–65.

ferent wages, and their corresponding labor-hours per man per unit of time. For example, MP_1 corresponds to the wage rate of OW_1, which gives a labor-hour rate of OH_1; MP_2 corresponds to OW_2 with a labor-hour rate of OH_2; and MP_3 corresponds to OW_3 with a labor-hour rate of OH_3. The curves in different positions show that a higher wage makes possible an increase in consumption, which in turn makes it possible for a worker to have a higher marginal product. Consequently, at a higher wage rate, the marginal-product curve is initially higher than that which exists at a lower wage. But this higher marginal productivity declines more rapidly because, given a total output to be produced, the aggregate number of workers required to accomplish the task decreases as the wage rate rises (or increases as the wage rate falls).

For each wage per man, and the corresponding labor-hours per man, there is an equilibrium employment point on the relevant marginal-product curve. Referring now to figure 2, at the equilibrium point of E_1, each worker receives the wage rate of OW_1 and works at the labor-hour rate of OH_1, and the total number of workers employed is ON_1. At the equilibrium point of E_2, each worker receives the wage rate of OW_2 and works at the OH_2 rate, and the total number of workers employed is ON_2. Note that ON_2 is smaller than ON_1, reflecting the fact that for the wage rate of OW_1 more workers are required than at the higher wage rate of OW_2. If the total number of workers available is ON_1, and the total number of workers employed is ON_2, the number of openly

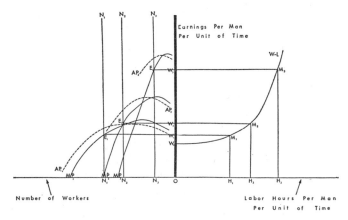

FIG. 2. Earning-productivity relationship of self-supporting family labor.

unemployed workers is ON_1 minus ON_2; in this impersonal labor market, they are the workers about whose economic state employers will not care.

It should be added that the possibilities of sharing by employed workers with their unemployed relatives and friends would not arise, for, first, there is no extended family-clan-village in this capitalistic (model) society, and, second, the wage received by the employed worker is only a biological minimum. In this connection it should also be noted that the marginal productivity of employed workers is positive, and not zero or negative. A marginal-product curve corresponding to the life-subsistence level, and to any wage rate below the minimum, for that matter, cannot be drawn because no one is capable of working at these low wages. Employers would not hire anyone who is physically incapable of contributing to total output. It is, therefore, in the self-interest of employers to prevent the marginal product (and the wage) from falling to or below the minimum. Indeed, it is in the employers' self-interest to prevent the wage rate from falling below OW_2. This means that, insofar as an employed worker is concerned, he has a positive marginal productivity above OW_2. Clearly, the concept of disguised unemployment does not apply to these employed workers. It will now be shown that neither does it apply to employed workers in tradition-directed societies.

THE SYSTEM OF EMPLOYMENT IN A TRADITION-DIRECTED SOCIETY

The assumptions made in the preceding hypothetical analysis of the impersonal social organization—worker homogeneity, no dependents, similarity of workers' economic conditions, and the productivity-consumption relationships—also apply to the tradition-directed society. But here there is no rigid employer-employee relation, nor does the principle of profit maximization by means of using as few workers as possible apply. All the available workers are absorbed into economic activity; and the total available work is shared among the workers. Consequently, family labor as a whole will become underemployed as compared with wage-workers.

In what manner does this process of absorption of family labor into work take place? Can the process of family labor pushing employment more and more, at a relatively high wage (say, W_2), *and at the same labor-hours per man*, continue until the marginal productivity of the worker reaches zero (e.g., toward N_1), still leaving some of the family workers completely idle?

Additional employment of workers (say, along MP_2) would increase total output to the point where the marginal product of labor becomes zero. But, as the labor-hours per man must be the same all along the marginal-product curve, the additional workers would consume as much as do other workers, and would consume more than they add to total output, leaving smaller and smaller savings for necessities of the coming year's operation (e.g., seed, fertilizer, repair and replacement of some capital goods). This necessity for some savings could impose a limitation upon the total product maximization with a relatively high earning per worker. Indeed, total output may not be enough even to pay the wage bill (say, OW_2 multiplied by ON_1) if the average productivity of workers at the employment level where the marginal productivity is zero is lower than the wage rate associated with the marginal-product curve (MP_2).

The solution—a constrained total product maximization with total wage bill less than total output—will become more difficult when there still are workers who are completely idle. The unemployed family members who have nowhere to go will be given a portion of the total output, further reducing savings which are necessary for the coming year's cultivation. But the possibility of an unconditional automatic apportioning of the family's total output cannot seriously be entertained. As long as the worker stays with the rest of his family and shares in their output, he will be obliged to share in the work.[8]

With a certain limitation imposed on the levels of total output and consumption by the necessity of providing savings for the coming year's cultivation, the sharing of employment among more workers than before means that the typical family will find a new

---

[8] Berdj Kenadjian, "Disguised Unemployment in Underdeveloped Countries" (unpublished Ph.D. dissertation, Harvard University, 1957), p. 55, points out difficulties in Lewis' view on unconditional sharing: "The assumption that Lewis makes about the way the product is shared in the subsistence sector—everyone getting an equal share *whether they work or not*—seems hard to believe" (italics added).

marginal-product curve given by MP_1, say, in figure 2. The marginal productivity of labor at a lower earning rate (W_1), with less labor-hours per man than in the previous situation (that is, W_2 wage rate and H_2 labor-hour rate), is no longer zero at that level of employment of workers (N_1) where the marginal productivity of labor was previously zero.

In short, the zero marginal productivity of labor will come quickly when few workers are employed or if the labor-hour rate is high. It will come slowly when a large number of workers are employed or if the labor-hour rate is low. Given a specified number of workers, the zero marginal productivity of labor with less than "full employment" will disappear when wage rates and labor-hours per man are reduced as a result of "full employment." Consequently, the concept of a zero marginal productivity of employed labor in this tradition-directed family system loses its usefulness in explaining the existence of surplus labor or disguised unemployment.[9]

Nevertheless, it is believed that the concept of disguised unemployment could be related to a zero marginal productivity of labor employed. If some of the workers were "removed" from the land, the wage rate of the remaining workers would have to be raised to obtain the same total amount of labor effort. The work force to be "removed" would then be surplus or disguised unemployment.

The important question at this point is: Could some of the family workers be simply removed from the land without any problems? Specifically, would the family workers be indifferent to a choice between family employment and wage employment in nonrural areas for a given wage rate?

At a given wage rate, preference for work over leisure may vary under different social and economic conditions. The social institutions, such as the family-clan-village systems, religious attachment, and so forth, may weaken the attraction of wage employment. On the other hand, extreme poverty may encourage the people to move away for alternative work. Thus, labor that may

---

[9] It could be, of course, that more than N_1 workers need to be employed. So long as the average product, after allowances for other costs, is slightly above OW_0, the traditional family system may, in the short run, employ workers irrespective of their marginal product.

be available in one society at a particular wage may not be available at the same wage in other societies.

Arthur Lewis, K. N. Raj, Rosenstein-Rodan, and Riesman have expressed their views on the removability of labor from the land. Lewis points out that workers would not give up family farming unless the alternative (wage employment) brought sufficient additional remuneration to offset the advantages of the prevailing system. If such remuneration was higher than what they would have to give up, family labor would give up family farming for wage employment. Conversely, those who are employed for wages would give up the employment and return to the family farm where a certain minimum scale of living is available to them, if the remuneration from wages was no better than what they would have earned had they remained on the farm.[10]

Rosenstein-Rodan, in an attempt to measure disguised unemployment, classified it as "removable" and "not removable" surplus labor.[11] Riesman, in a passage from *The Lonely Crowd*, also lends support to our point of view: ". . . the individual in a society dependent on tradition-direction . . . 'belongs'—he is not 'surplus,' as the modern unemployed are surplus, nor is he expendable as the unskilled are expendable in modern society. But by very virtue of his 'belonging,' life goals that are *his* in terms of conscious choice appear to shape his destiny only to a very limited extent, just as only to a limited extent is there any concept of progress for the group." [12]

The foregoing analysis leads us to consider the main thesis of this chapter—that the manpower surplus in underdeveloped countries can realistically be understood if it is classified as technical (removable) and tradition-directed (not removable) surplus labor. To focus the problem, we impose on our study a strict *ceteris paribus* assumption. Among other considerations, it is necessary that the estimate of surplus labor be based on a norm for the particular country or area concerned.

---

[10] Lewis, *op. cit.;* see also Raj, *op. cit.*

[11] P. N. Rosenstein-Rodan, "Disguised Unemployment and Underemployment in Agriculture," *Monthly Bulletin of Agricultural Economics and Statistics*, VI (July-Aug., 1957).

[12] David Riesman *et al., The Lonely Crowd: A Study of the Changing American Character* (New Haven: Yale University Press, 1950), p. 12.

SURPLUS LABOR FURTHER CONSIDERED, UNDER
A RELAXATION OF THE VARIOUS ASSUMPTIONS
IN OUR MODEL

The employment situations of the two apparently contrasting social arrangements have been compared without giving much consideration to the method and the organization of production in the two divergent societies. Although the mere availability of certain factors of production, such as land, labor, and skill, is assumed to be the same in both setups, landownership, the size of landholdings, and the availability of capital, for instance, should not be assumed to be the same for both. These differences, however, do not invalidate the comparison of the two setups for our purposes. As the conjectural social revolution is assumed to take place instantaneously, our analysis need not embrace patterns of change beyond what has been presented; further economic and social ramifications of the change to so different a mode of production would be of a long-run, dynamic nature.

On the other hand, a simplified model admittedly does not fit exactly the actual labor structures in underdeveloped countries; the work force is, in reality, heterogeneous, consisting partly of self-supporting family labor and partly of wage labor. As wageworkers in a tradition-dominated society are usually marginal (both socially and economically), and as any underemployment of this category of workers must be attributed to the lack of technical means of production rather than to traditional social institutions, the existence of wageworkers in prevailingly rural societies necessitates making a distinction between idle labor due to technical inadequacies and labor idle only in a tradition-directed sense.

If the assumption that these workers have no dependents is relaxed, it follows that a worker who has to support more dependents than another, other things being equal, will have more difficulty in remaining a part of the traditional social world. As a consequence, he is quite likely to become a marginal individual and seek wage employment elsewhere in order to improve his income. When such a worker fails to find wage employment elsewhere, he remains potentially withdrawable (from the land) and, compared with the employed wageworker, he is technically under-employed, but not underemployed in the tradition-directed sense.

If the assumption is relaxed that the farm workers under the traditional social arrangement are all equally situated econom-ically, those family workers who have little technical means of production, such as land, animals, tools, and the like, would be more underemployed than the workers of other family units who are better situated. As in the case of workers who have relatively more dependents than others, the underemployment of these family workers may be technical, rather than tradition-directed.

Furthermore, the possibility of permanent removal and of trans-ferring workers to an urban area depends upon the seasonal peak requirement for labor. If there is chronic open unemployment—excess labor over and above the peak requirement—it can be with-drawn with few problems. If, however, there is no chronic open unemployment, but only seasonal unemployment, then permanent removal of the unemployed is impossible. Such removal would require some changes in order to take care of the peak seasonal demand. This would be incompatible under the *ceteris paribus* assumption.[13] Nevertheless, in off seasons the mobilization of labor for economic development projects near the villages would be possible under the *ceteris paribus* assumption. It is important to note that some seasonally unemployed workers, although not re-movable permanently from the land, could be thus mobilized with-out creating a basic problem.

When the volume of removable labor is estimated, seasonal un-employment should be treated differently and separately from chronic unemployment. Once we admit the existence of seasonal unemployment (under the capitalistic social setup), the total number of workers required, including workers who are necessary to supplement the labor supply in peak agricultural seasons and who would be idle in off seasons, must be more than ON_3 workers in figure 2 (assuming that ON_3 workers are fully and continuously employed throughout the year). Let us say that the number of workers required is ON_2. Then, while ON_3 workers are fully em-ployed, ON_2 minus ON_3 workers are only occasionally fully em-

[13] Rosenstein-Rodan, however, does not adhere to this strict *ceteris paribus* assump-tion (*op. cit.*, p. 4).

ployed. As a result, removable surplus labor equals the total number of existing workers (ON_1) minus ON_2 workers, instead of ON_1 minus ON_3.

It should be noted here that the necessity for some savings as a hedge against possible unemployment during off seasons complicates the analysis, for, as is the case in sharing income with dependents, the link between earnings and labor effort will be broken. If this is so, workers must earn more than necessary for a particular level of labor effort. The unemployment during off seasons in this situation is primarily due to the insufficient technical means of production rather than to consumption itself.

The above analysis, in regard to the capitalistic social arrangement, suggests the possibility of seasonal underemployment in the traditional social arrangement. The seasonality of agriculture prevails among different types of social arrangements. Therefore a certain amount of seasonal (or technical) underemployment exists under the traditional social arrangement as well.

Because of the variations arising from relaxation of the rigid assumptions in the model, it is more realistic to consider underemployment in two classifications: technical underemployment and tradition-directed underemployment. Technical underemployment is true surplus labor when it is nonseasonal (or chronic); tradition-directed underemployment is not true surplus labor even when it is chronic.

CONCLUSION

The traditional school of thought on this subject has asserted a priori the zero marginal productivity of some employed labor, and the existence of removable surplus labor from the land under the assumption of *ceteris paribus.* In traditional thinking the notion of disguised unemployment is the core of the theory of so-called overpopulation. In other words, the extent of so-called overpopulation is directly derived from the productivity of labor: when the population is too large compared with the available land and capital, the marginal productivity of employed labor could be zero, or there could exist removable surplus labor. This theory does not tell us specifically why rural areas are more overpopulated than urban areas. But, as has been shown, under the given economic conditions the most plausible reason for rural overpopulation is the primary importance of the traditional social institutions, particularly the dole system, or sharing in the output. To work or not to work, however, is an important choice for a person to make. The choice is governed by his scale of values and the availability of work. The proponents of the concept of disguised unemployment have overlooked this important aspect of the individual utility function, and have failed to distinguish between technical idle labor and tradition-directed idle labor. Moreover, they have not made adequate allowance for household activities which constitute much of the productive effort in underdeveloped countries. People there produce most of the household goods and services which, in economically advanced countries, are objects of exchange in the market. Without making an adequate allowance for this sphere of productive activity, it is misleading to make an a priori case for the zero marginal productivity of any labor, or an a priori case for removable surplus labor.

In our model, a comparison is made with respect to the contrasting systems of employment in two apparently distinct social arrangements. It is observed that, under a social arrangement based on the capitalistic system, underemployment is not likely to occur. Employers try to use a worker as fully as possible, as long as it is profitable to do so, and the system of payment is based on the marginal productivity of the worker. In the tradition-directed society, in which open unemployment is not acceptable, underemployment is characteristic, and the system of earning is based on the practice of sharing.

We have deduced in our model that the openly unemployed under the hypothetical capitalistic society would be true surplus labor (of the technical type), but that current underemployment under the traditional social arrangement is not true surplus labor (of the technical type). The advocates of the concept of disguised unemployment have overlooked the essential significance of the function of the traditional value system. We have also shown that the marginal productivity of employed workers could not be zero under either type of social arrangement.

If the unrealistic assumptions in our model are relaxed, some technical underemployment must be admitted to exist in the tradition-directed society. Therefore, underemployment is not always tradition-directed from a more realistic point of view.

The relative proportion of tradition-directed and technical underemployment has important policy implications. Technical underemployment is true (or removable) surplus labor when it is chronic, but tradition-directed underemployment is not true surplus labor even when it is chronic, under the *ceteris paribus* assumption.

IV

Measurement of Underemployment

Labor Available and Labor Employed

In the last two chapters we examined the problem of surplus labor in underdeveloped countries in its so-called disguised unemployment forms and as underemployment. Inaccurate treatment of this subject in the past has confused and complicated the concept and has exaggerated the volume of true surplus labor. A new theoretical formulation is needed in order to make the concept valid and to measure accurately the amount of withdrawable surplus labor. In this, and in the next chapter, a case study of the Korean farm household is presented to test our own model. The main purpose in this chapter is to find a reliable standard for the measurement of withdrawable surplus labor. The next chapter will be concerned with its actual measurement.

We shall, first, discuss the methodological difference between the traditional method, which is based on the Nurkse concept of disguised unemployment, and an alternative method that we shall present and use. Second, we shall discuss the nature and the limitations of our sample and shall present a capsule view of the Korean farm household. The latter will be a preliminary step toward the measurement of "labor available" and "labor employed," and will constitute the third and last part of this chapter.

INDIRECT AND DIRECT METHODS
OF MEASURING SURPLUS LABOR

There are two main approaches to measuring surplus labor. The first approach may be called the indirect (or norm) method; the second approach, the direct method. The former, adopted by the traditional school, uses the standard of labor productivity to measure labor surplus. Generally speaking, the net amount of surplus labor arrived at by the indirect method is the actual labor available for farming minus the norm. According to Rosenstein-Rodan, there are three variants of this norm: (1) The amount of labor required to produce a given output may be a norm, which would then be subtracted from the amount of labor available to arrive at the volume of surplus labor. (2) The necessary density of population for a given type of cultivation may be a norm, which would then be deducted from the actual density of population to arrive at the extent of surplus labor. For these two variants, conversion coefficients of arable equivalents are used for different degrees of land fertility: for example, 1 hectare of garden equals 3 hectares of cultivated area, 1 hectare of meadow equals 0.4 hectares of cultivated area, and so on.[1] (3) The amount of labor required under a given type of cultivation to provide one person with a standard income may also be a norm. This may be compared with the amount of land and the agricultural population available to arrive at the size of the landless population, or the "surplus population." In this last method, conversion coefficients of standard-crop equivalents, or "crop units," are used.[2]

Perhaps the following quotation on this subject from Moore's study of eastern and southern Europe will illustrate a typical indirect method:

Under the assumption that a European average standard is reasonable, the countries of Eastern and Southern Europe have a surplus agri-

---

[1] See J. Poniatowski, "Population and Agriculture," in International Institute of Agriculture, *European Conference on Rural Life* (Geneva, 1939), quoted by P. N. Rosenstein-Rodan, "Disguised Unemployment and Underemployment in Agriculture," *Monthly Bulletin of Agriculture Economics and Statistics,* VI (July-Aug., 1957), 2.

[2] Wilbert E. Moore, *Economic Demography of Eastern and Southern Europe* (Geneva: League of Nations, 1945), pp. 53–69; Rosenstein-Rodan, *op. cit.,* p. 2.

cultural population of 45 per cent. By the same standard, the Southwestern peninsulas have a redundant farm population of 23 per cent. This means that with no increase in production a substantial proportion of the rural population would have to find other employment in order for the remainder to achieve a European average level, or, approximately that of Estonia.[3]

Although Rosenstein-Rodan recognizes the fact that the indirect method is not satisfactory, he rejects it solely on the technical ground that its results are highly imprecise because of the difficulties inherent in establishing a criterion of need.[4] We reject the indirect method not only because of this impreciseness, but primarily because of our objection to the traditional productivity criterion he borrows. The productivity criterion and the consequent indirect method, if adopted, would lead to (1) a surplus labor estimate that would be inaccurate and exaggerated for decision making on development programing or policies, and (2) a surplus labor force all of which could not be withdrawn from the land. The indirect method would be unreliable for workable decisions because of the fact that the particular country to which a norm from outside had been applied could have entirely different social and economic conditions from those of the norm country. It might be impossible to withdraw a significant part of the surplus labor without vitiating the *ceteris paribus* assumption, for the indirect method fails to recognize the difference between open (technical) and closed (tradition-directed) underemployment, and that the latter is not removable surplus labor.

Rosenstein-Rodan's direct method is based on two main calculations: "labor force" and "labor required." He does not, however, clearly explain the meaning of "labor required." "Labor required" could mean either the amount of labor actually employed or the amount of labor necessary for farming which is estimated without using a norm from outside. If the latter is true, detailed inquiries are required not only into different types of cultivation, different sizes and types of farm land, and the composition of the work force, but also into the location of land with respect to access to water and the work capacity of laborers, which may differ

---

[3] Moore, *op. cit.*, pp. 62–63.
[4] Cf. Rosenstein-Rodan, *op. cit.*, p. 2.

on different landholdings. Thus, immense difficulties and complications are inevitable in estimating labor required.

In this study a direct method is used, based on two main estimates: the measurement of "labor available" and of "labor employed." These are estimated on the basis of a sample study of Korean agriculture. Labor employed represents the amount of labor actually put into agricultural activity; it has nothing to do with any norm. It is estimated on the basis of an actual statistical investigation.

The direct method differs further from the one Rosenstein-Rodan used in his Italian agricultural study. He did not include wage labor in measuring surplus labor; consequently, he underestimated the total amount of surplus labor. The direct method takes into account both self-supporting and wage labor.

SURVEY DATA

The data required for this study were supplied by the research departments of the Bank of Korea, the Korean Agricultural Bank, and the Ministry of Agriculture and Forestry of the Korean government. Because the Korean economy is largely agricultural, permanent machinery has been set up by the government to make an annual investigation into agricultural conditions. This information is collected monthly by means of account books and of questionnaires answered by the respondents under the supervision of one part-time employee in each village, selected from among the people in that village.

In designing the sample study, 60 small administrative farm districts (*myun*) were selected. From these 60 farm districts, 600 farm units were selected.[5] The sampling units were selected by the stratified proportional random sampling method. As Korea is a very small country, all the districts are treated as a single homo-

---

[5] In 1959 there were 1,412 *myun* and 2,256,161 farm households, of which full-time farm households whose incomes were obtained solely through farming constituted 90 per cent. In part-time farm households, which constituted the remaining 10 per cent, a family member was engaged in nonagriculture, but the principal income was derived from farming (Korea, Ministry of Agriculture and Forestry, *Year Book of Agriculture and Forestry*, 1960 [Seoul, 1960], p. 5).

geneous area with respect to climatic and agricultural conditions.[6] From each district villages were selected at random and weighted in proportion to their farm population. All the farm households in the selected villages were divided into five groups for each district, according to the size of holdings. From each group farm units were again selected at random and weighted in proportion to farm population. By this procedure, a total of 600 farm households was selected throughout Korea. As of the end of 1959, about 98 per cent of all farm households in Korea were engaged in cereal farming. For this reason the sample inquiry covered only cereal farming. The population of the sample does not represent those farm households specializing in growing fruit or nuts, or in raising livestock and poultry.

The Bureau of Statistics in the Ministry of Home Affairs adopted the following criteria in defining farm households:

1) holding croplands of 300 *pyong* (300 *pyong* equals 0.245 acres) or more
2) raising 30 or more hens, ducks, and/or rabbits
3) breeding 3 or more cows, horses, and/or pigs
4) breeding one or more milk cows and/or goats for producing milk
5) maintaining one or more greenhouses
6) keeping five or more beehives
7) selling farm products of 100,000-*hwan* value or more in the period covered (1,000 *hwan* equaled $1.00 in 1959)

In our measurement of true surplus labor we have used only the first criterion for defining a farm household. Our sample does not include institutional farms, nor does it include persons who have small landholdings but whose principal income is derived from non-agricultural employment such as forestry, fishing, or trading.

Table 1 shows the sample distribution of farm households and related data by size of cultivated landholdings. The sample size, 582, is an average monthly figure. In January and February the planned sample of 600 was reported, but thereafter the number

---

[6] This method is valid only for a small country such as Korea, where the climatic conditions in different sections of the country do not vary enough to cause a significant difference in crop variety. The method is not applicable to the mainland of China, to India, or to other large countries.

TABLE 1

SAMPLE DISTRIBUTION, CULTIVATED LAND PER HOUSEHOLD AND AVERAGE
NUMBER OF HOUSEHOLD MEMBERS, BY FARM SIZE, KOREA,[a] 1959

Size of holding (in acres)	Size of sample	Cultivated land per household[b] (in acres)	Average number of household members[c]
1.225 and under	227	1.016	5.32
1.225–2.450	194	1.847	6.39
2.450–3.675	81	3.102	7.43
3.675–4.900	46	4.212	8.40
4.900 and above	34	6.056	8.63
Total or average	582	2.122	6.40

[a] 60 farm districts, 582 farms.
[b] This includes paddy fields and dry fields only. The mulberry orchards owned by those with farms of less than 1.225 acres amounted to about 0.00082 acres per household; for farms of more than 0.056 acres, about 0.0228 acres per household.
[c] Includes attached (hired) workers.
SOURCE: Bank of Korea, Research Department.

varied. About 72 per cent of the total households in the sample owned farms of less than 2.45 acres. The size of the family (including attached workers) tends to increase with an increase in farm size. It is evident, however, that the increase in farm size is greater than the accompanying increase in the size of the family. As a result, the ratio of size of family to landholding tends to decrease with the increase in farm size.[7]

Farms in Korea may be considered mostly family farms.[8] The

[7] As noted in chapter ii, this condition has allegedly been interpreted as a sign of disguised unemployment. It must be reëmphasized that the orthodox interpretation is not correct because, among other reasons, the technical means of production are more easily available on large farms than on small ones, and the average output per unit of land is greater on small farms than on large ones. John Lossing Buck's study on China, as well as Hoon Koo Lee's study on Korea and Shiroshi Nasu's study on Japan, must be interpreted more carefully so as to prevent the picture of employment conditions in these areas from being distorted. These three studies were all carried out under the auspices of the Institute of Pacific Relations. As the last two are not well known, it is Buck's study that laid the groundwork for the productivity criterion for disguised unemployment (Hoon Koo Lee, *Land Utilization and Rural Economy in Korea* [Chicago: University of Chicago Press, 1936]; Shiroshi Nasu, *Land Utilization in Japan* [Chicago: University of Chicago Press, 1929]; John Lossing Buck, *Land Utilization in China* [Chicago: University of Chicago Press, 1937]).

[8] The prevalence of family farms in an agricultural area, is, however, not a sufficient condition for establishing a case for disguised unemployment. For example,

main supply of labor for cultivation comes from the family. It will, therefore, be useful to start our investigation with an examination of family size and the number of workers per farm household. Table 2 shows the distribution of the sample population by age and occupation. Nonfarming activities occupy about 3.04 persons per household, out of a total of 6.40 persons in the average family. The rest of the family, 3.36 persons, are occupied in farming. Children and students constitute most of the nonfarming group. Only 0.34 persons are employed solely in household maintenance, and 0.06 persons are engaged in wage and salary employment outside the home. On the average, 0.13 persons out of 6.40 are hired hands (or attached wageworkers).

TABLE 2

FARM FAMILIES BY AGE AND OCCUPATION, AVERAGE PER FARM HOUSEHOLD, KOREA,[a] 1959

	Nonfarming				Farming		
Age group	Pre-school children	School students	House-hold	Others[b]	Family hands[c]	Hired hands[d]	Total
14 and under	1.42	1.04	0.02	0.00	0.05	—	2.53
15–19	—	0.17	0.05	0.00	0.43	0.03	0.68
20–49	—	0.01	0.08	0.05	2.06	0.09	2.29
50–59	—	—	0.02	0.01	0.43	0.01	0.47
60 and above	—	—	0.17	0.00	0.26	0.00	0.43
Total[e]	1.42	1.22	0.34	0.06	3.22	0.13	6.40

[a] 60 farm districts, 582 farms.
[b] Includes nonfarm wage laborers and nonfarm salaried employees.
[c] Includes self-employed and wage laborers, who are principally engaged in farming on their own or on somebody else's land.
[d] Refers only to those employed by the sample family.
[e] Because of rounding, individual figures do not necessarily add up to total.
SOURCE: Bank of Korea, Research Department.

A clear-cut occupational classification of farm families is not easy to make. The nonfarming family members often help the farm hands, especially in busy seasons, and vice versa in off sea-

about 67 per cent of the farms in the United States are family farms (see Marshall Harris and Robert A. Rohwer, *Family Farming*, National Planning Association, Planning Pamphlet no. 99 [July, 1957], pp. 1, 16).

sons. A clear-cut line between household activity and farm work is particularly difficult to draw. In the Korean survey this problem was handled with great care; specific directions were given to the surveyors on each type of situation. For example, running errands and going to market were treated as household work, whereas looking after cattle and driving carts were included in farming. Although some arbitrary decisions about occupational classification of family members were inevitable, the classification used should serve as a useful guide and as a basis for estimating the amount of labor available for farming. The amount of labor available is quite different from the number of farm hands available, as shown in table 2.

MEASURING AVAILABLE LABOR

To estimate the amount of labor available, the following assumptions and definitions have been used:

1) *Active population.*—The active population includes those between 15 and 59 years of age. Persons outside this age range are classified as *inactive population,* because their chance of employment in alternative work is slight. In our sample, of the 6.40 persons per farm household, 3.44 persons are in the active category and 2.96 are in the inactive category. The Japanese government, in estimating the labor force of Korea in 1927, used the age range from 15 to 45 for women and from 15 to 50 for men.[9] John Lossing Buck, who studied Chinese agriculture in 1937, considered 15 to 59 as the age range of the working population in farming.[10] Rosenstein-Rodan defined the active population in his Italian study as those from 15 to 65 years of age. For Korea we exclude from the active population the age groups of 14 and under and 60 and above. The low physical strength, skill, and literacy of these people limit the scope of their utilization in other than very light and simple farm work. Even if these people were considered as labor available for work, the effective number of persons who could be withdrawn, after subtracting those who would be attend-

---

[9] Eisuke Zensho, *Chosen no Jinko Kensyo* [*Population Phenomena of Korea*] Chosa Siryo, no. 22 (Seoul: Chosen-So-Tokoo-Hoo [Chosen Publishing Co.], 1927), pp. 186–187.

[10] Buck, *op. cit.,* p. 294.

ing school and those largely physically incapable of working, would inevitably be very small.

2) *Farm workers.*—Farm workers are those of the active population who are principally engaged in farming. This definition therefore excludes those who attend school and those who are engaged principally in household duties and other nonfarming occupations. Family farm workers include self-employed family workers and attached workers. The farm owner works mainly for his own benefit, whereas the latter work for wages on annual contract. It must be noted, however, that the family farm worker also occasionally works for wages or exchanges labor with others, especially in busy seasons; but he is mainly engaged in his own farming.

The "agricultural laborer," defined by the Indian government as one who works outside his own farm for more than one-half of his yearly working days, is regarded in our sample mainly as an attached worker.[11] The casual or day laborer also has his own land, and therefore does not work outside his own farm for more than one-half of his working time or his income. The amount of labor put in outside one's own farm, however, increases as the farm size decreases, although it seldom goes beyond the one-half limit. Those who have to work outside their own farms more than one-half the time prefer, if there is no alternative employment, to work as attached labor, as this is more secure than casual labor. This is one of the characteristics of rural employment in Korea. Casual labor is relatively insignificant in Korean agriculture. If one must work outside his own farm for more than one-half of his time or income, and if one is not an attached worker, he is mainly employed in occupations other than farming. This category of worker comprises 0.06 persons per household (see table 2); these must be excluded from the estimate of farm workers.

We also exclude from the active population, in order to arrive at the correct number of farm workers, those who attend school and those who maintain the household. The exclusion of those who attend school presents no problem; but the number required to carry out the household activities must be carefully considered.

---

[11] For the definition of agricultural labor, see India, Ministry of Labour, *Agricultural Labour Enquiry: Report on Intensive Survey of Agricultural Labour,* I (Delhi, 1955), 37.

Because the household constitutes the major productive unit in Korea, producing most of the goods and services that, in more advanced countries, are objects of exchange in the market place, a reduction in the volume of household goods and services would result if an unreasonable number of people were withdrawn from such a farm household. We assume that, on the average, 1.3 women per household are required to perform household tasks.[12] Because traditional Korean housekeeping involves many time-consuming and painstaking duties—refining and crushing grain; the traditional cooking, washing, and clothes making; and long trips for marketing—the allocation of 1.3 women per household for these activities is not excessive.

The refining and crushing of grain in preparing it for cooking are still common activities in the rural household. The preparation of meals three times a day is a more time-consuming task than in economically advanced countries. All three meals are usually prepared with fresh food (not canned or preserved). Boiled rice or barley is served at all three meals, so that the preparation of breakfast, lunch, and dinner is almost equally time-consuming. The primitive method of washing clothes by beating them is also a lengthy process, and tiring work for women. Making clothes is perhaps the most time-consuming task of all; in rural areas all women's clothes and most men's clothes are homemade. Each time clothes are washed they are separated (ripped) into their original parts, washed by beating, dried with starch, beaten again, and finally resewn into their original shape; this process of separating and resewing clothes has been going on for centuries. One reason for this procedure is that the primitive method of washing and stretching clothes would tear and twist the seams and lining; this is looked down upon by Korean women who take great pride in the needlework of their hand-sewn clothes.

If, because of prevailing customs, some women are not willing to accept work outside the household—either on their own farms or in wage employment—they should not be included in the number of farm workers available. In rural Korea, for instance,

---

[12] Rosenstein-Rodan (*op. cit.*, p. 3) assumes that a family of five members or less requires one woman house worker, that two women are needed for families from six to ten persons, and that families of more than ten persons require three women house workers.

unmarried young women in even moderately well-to-do families (perhaps in farm households having more than 2.45 acres of cultivated land) fit into this category. But it must be noted that, as these young women are, in fact, engaged in various important household activities, they need not be excluded as active members of the family in our estimate of farm workers. In other words, our allotment of 1.3 women has already taken care of these unavailable (for farming) but active members of the family.

The remainder, after all these exclusions of inactive members of the family outside the 15–59 age range—those attending school, those in nonfarm employment, and active women who are required to maintain the household—is the number of farm workers available. This number is, on the average, 1.90 persons per family of 6.4 persons.

3) *Workdays available.*—These are estimated at 280 a year for men and 268 for women. Leisure time is roughly determined by climatic conditions, institutional holidays, and, of course, the physical condition of the worker. Although there are no rigidly fixed workdays, the estimated 280 days for men (see table 11, p. 74) average out to approximately 5.5 days per week. In estimating workdays available, a difficult problem is posed by climatic conditions such as freezing weather, snow, and monsoons. Korean winters are so cold that the earth is mostly frozen, and little outdoor work can be done. Rosenstein-Rodan contends that such climatic conditions would substantially reduce the number of farm workdays available.[13] In reality, however, it is the labor employed, not the labor available, that is reduced by the climatic conditions. It is not that the laborers are incapable of carrying out the work because, for example, of physical weakness or lack of skill, but that climatic conditions prevent them from working. Therefore labor not used in inclement weather should not be entirely overlooked in measuring the amount of surplus labor, as alternative types of employment are not limited to outdoor work.

The 280 working-day norm is not much above Rosenstein-Rodan's 270-day norm in his Italian study, but it is less than Buck's 300-day norm in his Chinese study. The Indian Society of Agricultural Economics also took 300 days as a normal adult

---

[13] *Ibid.*, p. 3.

male working year.[14] Our figure is larger than Rosenstein-Rodan's mainly because farm workers are not unavailable in the severe winter or in rainy seasons; it is below that used by Buck and by the Indian Society of Agricultural Economics because we believe that our leisure criteria are more comprehensive. In any event, different countries are not exactly comparable with one another because weather conditions, social and family traditions, and the physical condition of the workers differ. In Korea, numerous social and family celebrations occur in the months of September, December, and January. There are fewer working days in September, for instance, because of harvest festivals, similar to Thanksgiving and other harvest holidays in Western countries.

4) *Hours available for work.*—Even when we have established the number of farm workers available and the number of working days available, we have not yet arrived at the figure for labor available, which is what we are seeking. The labor available, in our sense, requires an additional estimate of working hours per day. We have taken into account the effect of climatic conditions on working days available; the same does not apply to working hours available. That is to say, climatic conditions such as those mentioned by Rosenstein-Rodan cannot substantially reduce the working hours available, although they may possibly reduce the hours of work actually put into farming operations.

Computing women's farm working hours requires an additional qualification. Some kinds of work cannot be done by women, such as heavy loading and unloading, and heavy hauling when carts are not available. But most of the unutilized women's labor during the working day is not available for other purposes; it is not surplus labor. Therefore, the available working hours of women must be reduced to this extent.

An important criterion in this respect is the physical condition of the worker, which is here considered a measure of the major energy components of his food intake, that is, calories and protein. The average daily caloric intake in Korea is approximately 2,100 units; the protein consumption per capita is about 70 grams, of

---

[14] *Ibid.;* Buck, *op. cit.,* pp. 295–296; Indian Society of Agricultural Economics, "Employment of Manpower in Agriculture," in *Studies in Indian Agricultural Economics,* ed. J. P. Bhattacharjee (Bombay, 1958), p. 235.

which about 14 per cent is of animal origin.[15] The peoples of relatively advanced countries consume from 30 to 60 per cent more food than Koreans (see table 3). The Italians in Rosenstein-Rodan's study consume substantially more food than Koreans—

TABLE 3

DAILY CALORIE AND PROTEIN INTAKE PER CAPITA

Country	Years	Calories	Protein (in grams)	Percentage protein of animal origin
Korea[a]	1959	2,100–2,200	70	14
China (Formosa)	1957	2,400	57	12
Ceylon	1957	2,110	43	4
India	1954–1956	1,890	50	6
Pakistan	1957–1958	2,010	49	10
Philippines	1954–1955	1,940	49	6
Turkey	1957–1958	2,890	93	9
Egypt[b]	1954–1958	2,570	75	11
Greece	1957–1958	2,650	85	12
Italy[b]	1958–1959	2,650	77	18
New Zealand	1957	3,370	104	49
Denmark	1957–1958	3,420	93	41
Switzerland	1957–1958	3,240	95	35
France	1957–1958	2,910	96	—
West Germany	1958–1959	2,990	80	33
United Kingdom	1957–1958	3,300	87	38
United States	1958	3,100	93	41

[a] Estimated in this study.
[b] Estimated by the Food and Agriculture Organization (FAO) of the United Nations.
SOURCES: Except for Korea, see United Nations, Department of Economic and Social Affairs, *Statistical Yearbook, 1959* (New York, 1959), pp. 296–301. For more detailed data on food consumption, see FAO, *Food Balance Sheets*, 2d issue, 1955, and FAO, *Review of Food Consumption Surveys* (Rome, 1958).

more by about 550 caloric units and about 7 grams of protein, or by about 6 and 10 per cent, respectively.

Calorie requirements vary according to age group, sex, and type of work performed. A rough estimate based on the age and

[15] See Chong-Keuk Song, "Some Food Problems in Korea," in *Theses Collection,* IV (Seoul: Chungang University, 1959), 174.

sex distribution of the Korean population indicates that the present caloric intake is insufficient for people doing heavier than "ordinary" work (see table 4). On the average, a woman requires about 15 to 20 per cent less than a man. Adolescents and young adults require the most, the amount needed decreasing about 2 to 3 per cent every ten years.[16]

TABLE 4

CALORIE AND PROTEIN REQUIREMENTS BY DEGREE OF LABOR

Degree of labor	Men		Women	
	Calories	Protein (in grams)	Calories	Protein (in grams)
Light	2,200	70	1,800	80
Ordinary	2,500	80	2,100	70
Heavy	3,000	95	2,400	75
Very heavy	3,500	110	2,800	85
Extremely heavy	4,000	120	—	—

SOURCE: Chong-Keuk Song, "Some Food Problems in Korea," in *Theses Collection,* IV (Seoul: Chungang University, 1959), 173.

The caloric intake by the active farm population is the residual after consumption by the inactive population. Mathematically, 2,100 calories $= \frac{1}{2}(1,700 + 2,500)$, where the fraction $\frac{1}{2}$ indicates roughly the proportion of active to inactive farm population, and 1,700 calories is taken as the average daily caloric intake of the inactive adult population. Twenty-five hundred calories per person are then left over for the active population. Assuming that the proportion of women farm workers to the total active population is $\frac{1}{2}$, and that a woman requires 2,400 calories daily in order to do heavy work, the number of calories left over per person for the active male population is 2,600 daily units. These 2,600 calories are insufficient for men doing heavy work. This difference in the consumption level should be reflected in the

[16] Up-to-date information on the Korean people's caloric and protein intake is not available. Prewar information provided by the Korean Department of Health and Welfare is available but cannot be used for a study of present conditions. The average daily caloric intake then was 2,000 units; protein intake was 60 grams, of which 9 grams was of animal origin (*ibid.*, p. 172).

hours of work available versus the hours of work actually employed.

Nevertheless, as the number of hours of work available, the rigid Western standard of eight hours per day has some meaning in our context. Workers in Western nations actually work more than eight hours a day if the work done within their households is included. But in our scheme of examining the possibility of withdrawing some labor from the land, it is impractical to assume that more than eight hours a day are available because of the lower caloric and protein intakes, and for other reasons. Rosenstein-Rodan's estimate of the hours of work available, ranging from eight to thirteen a day, is of dubious value for development programing. The monthly estimate of Rosenstein-Rodan does not

TABLE 5

MONTHLY HOME CONSUMPTION OF PRINCIPAL AGRICULTURAL PRODUCTS
PER HOUSEHOLD, KOREA,[a] 1959

Month	Rice[b]	Barley[b]	Other summer grains (wheat, etc.)[b]	Other grains[b]	Pulse (peas, beans, etc.)[b]	Potatoes[c]
January	609	82	19	49	51	6.5
February	640	70	26	50	39	3.5
March	611	110	24	50	21	9.6
April	627	139	29	45	15	8.3
May	501	178	36	47	32	3.4
June	381	357	38	44	63	2.7
July	250	414	79	24	18	5.9
August	196	414	93	17	8	4.8
September	251	374	65	15	19	4.0
October	560	349	78	14	24	6.3
November	627	148	28	23	59	7.2
December	639	96	13	33	133	7.4
Total	5,892	2,731	528	411	482	69.6

[a] 60 farm districts.
[b] Measured in *hop* (1 *hop* = .18 quart).
[c] Measured in *kwan* (1 *kwan* = 3.75 kilograms).
SOURCE: Bank of Korea, Research Department, *Economic Statistics Year Book*, 1960, p. 279.

reflect at all the differences in actual food consumption at different times of the year. A careful observation of the pattern of food consumption on the Korean farm (table 5) shows that food is relatively more available and that there is actually a higher consumption rate in slack seasons than in busy seasons. This is owing to the seasonal nature and the limited volume of agricultural output. This paradoxical condition would prevail in any poor farm community.

Farm family consumption is highest in November and December, for rice is most plentiful after the October harvest. Barley is harvested in May. The busiest season comes in June and July, when rice is transplanted; in this peak season, however, the farmer is provided with relatively inadequate food, both in quality and in quantity. Rice stocks have been greatly diminished, and the farmer's main food is barley. Thus an outstanding feature of the consumption pattern is that farmers cannot afford to eat enough at the time when they have to work hardest and longest. It is for this reason that the number of hours of work available per day in the peak season is not larger than in the off season.

An examination of total average food expenditures per household, in connection with their respective price indexes, also reveals lower food consumption in June and July. The relatively high price index would cause a reduction in the physical amount of food consumption. The unfavorable diet conditions for the peak months, June and July, may be deduced from table 6. Although food consumption in the summer peak season, June and July, is relatively low, the hours of work available are nevertheless assumed to be at least eight a day, as working conditions are much more pleasant than in the winter months.

The hours of work available in the winter need not be less because of shorter daylight and cold weather, as is assumed by Rosenstein-Rodan, because laborers can perform indoor work. But we do not assume that there are more hours of work than in the summer months, because more calories are needed in cold weather than in mild weather for an equivalent amount of work.[17]

It is assumed here that, as far as the hours available for work are concerned, there is no difference between men and women

---

[17] This is the suggestion of Charles L. Baldwin.

TABLE 6

AVERAGE MONTHLY FOOD EXPENDITURES IN KOREAN FARM HOUSEHOLDS,[a] 1959
(In *hwan*)

Month	Total	Grain	Subsidiary foods	Others	Wholesale price index of edible agricultural products (1955 = 100)
January	19,294	15,171	1,955	2,168	127.0
February	19,713	14,868	2,857	1,988	129.2
March	18,070	13,942	1,805	2,323	125.6
April	15,912	11,886	1,868	2,158	126.2
May	17,894	13,730	2,402	1,762	139.7
June	14,786	10,713	2,497	1,576	142.9
July	14,403	10,543	2,357	1,503	140.0
August	15,700	11,711	2,404	1,585	143.5
September	18,486	13,731	2,805	1,950	145.6
October	16,519	11,797	2,833	1,889	128.7
November	24,840	12,131	8,197	4,512	121.3
December	21,240	15,153	2,405	3,682	119.3
Total[b]	216,857	155,376	34,385	27,096	

[a] 60 farm districts.
[b] In cash: 41,914 *hwan*
In kind: 174,943 *hwan*
_____
Total: 216,857 *hwan*
SOURCE: Bank of Korea, Research Department, *Economic Statistics Year Book*, 1960, pp. 237, 283.

and among different age groups in the active population. Eight hours per day applies to every kind of farm worker. Women's periodic need for time off has been considered in our estimate of the number of days available for work: 280 days per year for men, 268 days per year for women. The difference in work capacity between the sexes and among different age groups, however, still remains to be considered.

5) *Coefficients of labor available.*—Coefficients are conventionally used to convert the labor of different age and sex groups into a standard man-equivalent. Even if the number of hours worked

by a woman, a child, or an aged person is the same as for a man, the amount of work accomplished will be less. It is assumed, therefore, that a male farm worker equals 1, a woman farm worker

TABLE 7

AVERAGE ADULT FARM WAGES[a] BY TYPE OF CULTIVATION, KOREA, 1959
(In *hwan*)

Type of cultivation	Male	Female	Ratio[b]
Daily wages[c]			
Transplanting	926	698	0.75
Weeding in paddy fields	961	634	0.66
Weeding in dry fields	821	522	0.64
Planting in paddy fields	958	[d]	[d]
Threshing rice	1,131	430	0.38
Planting in dry fields	912	[d]	[d]
Threshing barley	1,096	478	0.44
Seasonal wages			
	8,557	3,000	0.35
Annual wages[e]			
	70,912	[d]	[d]

[a] All wages are those paid to workers with full labor capacity (i.e., those from 20 to 50 years of age).
[b] Male wage = 1.
[c] The value of allowances as part of daily wages includes the amount paid for staple food, subsidiary food, tobacco, and alcoholic beverages.
[d] Data not available.
[e] The term of annual employment is 361 days. The value of allowances as part of annual wages includes the outlay for clothes and other miscellaneous expenses, such as for shoes and haircuts, and cash allowances paid on special fete days.
SOURCE: Korean Agricultural Bank, Research Department, *Agricultural Year Book*, 1960, sec. 3, pp. 174–175.

equals 0.6, and the inactive population, by definition, equals 0. As the amount of labor available varies with the value of the coefficient, it is appropriate to explain the criteria for establishing coefficients. Our basic criterion is the relative farm wage rate of men and women (tables 7, 8). It is assumed that women's labor power and skill are by and large reflected in the wage rate they receive. Some limitations to coefficients thus established must, however, be noted.

TABLE 8

Adult Farm Wages per Day, Korea, 1959

(In *hwan*)

Month	Without meal		One meal		Two meals		Three meals		Four meals		Five meals		Average		
	Male	Female	Male	Female	Male	Female	Male	Female	Male	Female	Male	Female	Male	Female	Ratio
May[a]	772	476	644	393	521	344	509	312	488	314	446	248	981	599	0.61
June	783	538	671	451	552	388	502	335	497	[b]	463	286	997	647	0.65
July	792	488	680	401	573	365	491	320	474	312	442	296	995	616	0.62
August	788	471	675	407	571	356	489	332	483	312	460	296	995	612	0.62
September	800	550	800	336	538	330	524	308	481	300	507	337	938	563	0.60
October	800	500	750	350	544	335	600	360	506	308	568	350	993	625	0.63
November	800	400	750	325	527	278	565	364	508	290	519	375	960	586	0.61
December	800	500	600	325	508	255	536	316	538	400	450	325	914	549	0.60
Average	792	490	696	374	542	331	527	331	497	319	482	314	972	599	0.62

[a] Data are unavailable for first four months of year.

[b] Data unavailable.

Source: Korean Agricultural Bank, Research Department, *Agricultural Year Book*, 1960, sec. 3, pp. 232–233.

a) Such a coefficient, derived from farm wage rates, is not necessarily so accurate in estimating the labor available for real capital formation as for farming. This is so because the types of work involved are quite different. Different types of work obviously require different skills and capacities, and the respective wage rate must vary accordingly. A comparison of the wage rate in the agricultural sector with that in other sectors of the economy (table 9) reveals that the ratio between female and male farm wage rates is higher than in other sectors (mining and manufacturing). This seems to imply that in the agricultural sector, as compared with other sectors, the demand for unskilled female labor is relatively high. In any event, this difference in the wage ratios is very

TABLE 9

AVERAGE DAILY WAGE RATES OF UNSKILLED WORKERS
IN PRINCIPAL SECTORS OF THE ECONOMY, KOREA
(In *hwan*)

Sector	Year[a]	Male	Female	Ratio
Agriculture	1959	972	599	0.62
Mining	1958	1,330	520	0.39
Manufacturing	1958	810	440	0.54

[a] As the wages are for different years, the figures are not comparable, but the ratios within each sector are still useful.
SOURCE: For agricultural data, see source for table 8; for mining and manufacturing, see Bank of Korea, Research Department, *Annual Economic Review*, 1959, sec. 3, pp. 288–290.

marked. Therefore the employment of women in alternative occupations may reduce the coefficient.

b) This problem also arises in regard to the different age groups of farm workers. Unfortunately, no data showing relative wage rates among different age and sex groups, other than adult wage rates, are available at the present time. We therefore did not attempt to establish detailed coefficients by further breaking down the 15–59 age group. Aside from the lack of data, several reasons argue against more detailed coefficients: (1) As about 71 per cent of all farm workers fall into the age group of those who receive the full-scale wage rate (those between 20 and 50 years of age), we assume that the wage data for this latter group are representative of the entire group (those between 15 and 59 years of age). (2) Furthermore, as we excluded the inactive population from the category of farm workers on the ground that their chance of employment in some alternative occupation is slight, the coefficient of 1 for the younger and older groups in the active population will somewhat offset the exclusion of the inactive population. (3) The coefficient of 1 for these younger and older age groups (within the 15–59 range) will not jeopardize the resulting volume (in percentages) of surplus labor, because the same coefficient for men, 1, and the same coefficient for women, 0.6, are applied to the calculation of the man-equivalent of labor employed. (4) Because of the allotment of a large number of women farm workers to household duties, the number of women available for farming proper is relatively small. As, therefore, there are few female farm workers, the effect of the coefficient is reduced proportionately.

Rosenstein-Rodan used for his Italian study the coefficient of 1 for the male workers from 19 to 65 years of age; the Department of Agriculture and Forestry in Japan used the coefficient of 1 for the Japanese male worker from 20 to 70 years of age. Our coefficient of 1 applies to male workers from 15 to 59 years old.[18] In every instance the age group delimited serves as a basis for the conversion of labor available (or labor employed) into man-equivalents. The range used here, from 15 to 59 years of age, is narrower by two years and six years, respectively, than those used in the other two studies. Therefore, a further breakdown of the age group in our study would substantially reduce the amount of labor available, in terms of its man-equivalent.

In estimating the coefficient of labor capacity between the sexes,

[18] (a) Rosenstein-Rodan's coefficients for "labor force":

Sex	Age			
	13 and under	14–18	19–65	66 and above
Male	0	0.5	1	0
Female	0	0.5	0.6	0

(b) The coefficients used by the Department of Agriculture and Forestry in Japan for "labor force":

Sex	Age			
	10–14	15–19	20–70	71 and above
Male	0.20	0.70	1.00	0.60
Female	0.20	0.70	0.80	0.40

(c) The coefficients for "labor force" used by the Industrial Development Committee of the Korean government:

Sex	Age					
	10–15	16–20	21–50	51–60	61–70	71 and above
Male	0.40	0.80	1.00	0.80	0.65	0.45
Female	0.35	0.65	0.80	0.65	0.50	0.30

SOURCES: For (a), Rosenstein-Rodan, *op. cit.*, pp. 3–4; for (b) and (c), Korean Agricultural Bank, Research Department, *Agricultural Year Book*, 1959, sec. 1, p. 70.

as well as among different age groups, the criterion of differential food consumption (in terms of calories and other properties of food) does not necessarily lead to a reliable picture of differential labor capacity. This is so because, for example, the female worker is physically weaker than the male, even when the same amount of food is provided for both. In other words, although the difference in food consumption between men and women in general is about 20 per cent, the difference in (crude) labor capacities is not necessarily correlated with the differential in food consumption, but is lower beyond the difference in food consumption. The Industrial Development Agency in Korea tentatively established a coefficient of 0.8 for the female age group between 21 and 50. Although the age grouping differs from ours, we believe that this coefficient of 0.8 overestimates the man-equivalent labor of this female age group. The criterion for the coefficient is obviously not the relative wage rate, but probably the differential in food consumption. This of course does not mean that the labor capacity within an age-sex group does not vary with differential food consumption. For example, the labor capacity of a Korean laborer must be substantially different from that of an American laborer, simply because of the difference in food consumption.

On the basis of the preceding explanation of active population, farm workers, days and hours available for work, and the coefficient of labor capacity, the determination of labor available which we are seeking is measured as shown in tables 11 and 12. Total labor available in table 12 equals total male labor available plus total female labor available. The total labor available for 1959 is the sum of all the monthly figures for that year. The monthly figures of labor available are computed by multiplying the numbers of farm workers available in the sample by the hours of labor available in a month.

MEASURE OF LABOR EMPLOYED

In order to know the extent of labor employed in the Korean agricultural community, the number of hours actually devoted to various activities was investigated in the sample inquiry. In this connection, four methodological considerations merit special attention:

1) In underdeveloped countries where agriculture predominates and productive units are organized on a family basis, there is no clear distinction between household activities and farming. There is also no clear distinction between those who are wholly out of work and those who are working only part of the time. Those who would otherwise be wholly out of work usually engage in household activities and continue to receive a share of the family income. It is for this reason that in our measurement of labor employed we do not use the number of farm workers employed. Instead, we use the amount of labor time in terms of hours of work actually done by the worker.

2) Data on the actual hours of work done, which were recorded each day, are arranged monthly for each category of the sample. The investigation of hours of work is confined to farming and does not include the hours of work spent in household activities. Farming, however, includes work done for wages on farms owned by others, as well as the kind of work deemed indispensable for farm operation, such as building community irrigation systems and dams. Furthermore, farming in our sense also includes other work performed by the farmer, some of which is compulsory labor, such as construction of highways near the village. The inclusiveness of our use of the term "farming" gives us a more accurate standard for measuring the volume of employment and underemployment (see appendix table 1).

3) In the survey, the various classifications of workers—self-supporting family workers, attached wageworkers, and casual wageworkers—are also broken down by sex and age groups (see appendix table 2).

4) The hours of work done by the "inactive" population and by women of the active age are converted into man-equivalent hours. This procedure is necessary in order to make the labor employed comparable with the labor available. The coefficient of labor employed for different age and sex groups is shown in table 10.

As noted in the discussion of the coefficient of labor available, the relative wage rates are assumed to reflect the labor capacities and skills possessed by different age and sex groups. The coefficient of one male farm worker in the 15–59 age range and the coefficient of one female farm worker in the same age range are figured

TABLE 10

Coefficients of Labor Used for Korean Workers Employed in Farming

Sex	Age		
	14 and under	15–59	60 and above
Male	0.3	1.0	0.6
Female	0.3	0.6	0.4

roughly on the ratio of their wage rates, that is, 1.0 to 0.6, respectively. Incidentally, Lee also figures a coefficient of 0.6 for Korean women.[19]

TABLE 11

Labor Available, Korea,[a] 1959

Month	Number of households in sample	Per worker						Number in total sample		
		Workdays available per month		Work hours available per day	Work hours available per month[b]		Man-equivalent of woman labor available per month[c]	Family farm workers available		Hired (attached) farm workers available
		Male	Female	Male and Female	Male	Female		Male	Female	Male
January	600	21	20	8	168	160	96.0	948	156	72
February	600	21	20	8	168	160	96.0	924	186	66
March	562	24	23	8	192	184	110.4	877	118	67
April	578	24	23	8	192	184	110.4	890	115	92
May	569	25	24	8	200	192	115.2	887	119	119
June	569	25	24	8	200	192	115.2	876	85	96
July	582	24	23	8	192	184	110.4	896	93	93
August	580	24	23	8	192	184	110.4	882	104	87
September	588	25	24	8	200	192	115.2	905	117	88
October	589	25	24	8	200	192	115.2	907	112	94
November	588	22	21	8	176	168	100.8	906	117	88
December	579	20	19	8	160	152	91.2	886	104	75
Total		280	268							

[a] 60 farm districts.

[b] The working hours available per month are computed by multiplying the work hours available per day by workdays available per month.

[c] The man-equivalent of woman labor is computed by multiplying the work hours of women available per month by 0.6, the coefficient of their labor capacity.

Source: Based on data provided by Bank of Korea, Research Department.

[19] Lee, *op. cit.*, p. 227.

The true coefficient of labor used can be established only by measuring differential labor efficiency for each different type of work. This procedure is necessary because much of the light work would have to be done by male farm workers if the inactive population and women farm workers were not available. There are many such jobs: for example, looking after animals and keeping sparrows away from crops. Animal husbandry in summertime is so simple that it is usually handled by children; it requires taking the animals to a place where there is grass and, after a while, bringing them home. Sparrow watching is also simple. Both these duties, however, are absolutely necessary and are important parts of the farming operation. In jobs like these, which are usually handled by the inactive population, the coefficient must be 1. But there are many other kinds of work for which the inactive population would need much more time, or which it simply cannot do, such as heavy hauling and plowing in the field. For these types of work, the coefficient must be at or near zero.

An establishment of coefficients for all the various kinds of work involved in farming is not possible on the basis of our present data. Therefore, the only method available for approximating the differentials in labor efficiency is to use an average of the ratios of the respective wage rates for each month (see table 8). The relatively higher ratio of women's wages to men's wages in June, July, August, and October reflects the greater availability of work that can be performed by women farm workers, such as the transplanting of rice, hoeing, weeding, reaping, and helping with the threshing. The coefficients of labor efficiency for those (the very young and the very old) who do not receive the full-scale wage rates cannot be established in the same manner because of lack of information.

Total labor employed (see table 12) equals the total male labor employed plus total female labor employed. The total labor employed for the year 1959 is the sum of all the monthly figures for that year. The monthly figures of labor hours employed come from the sample survey. The labor employed is the actual hours of work done by the active and the inactive population.

TABLE 12

LABOR AVAILABLE AND LABOR EMPLOYED EXPRESSED IN HOURS OF MAN-EQUIVALENT, KOREA,[a] 1959

Month	Family labor available			Attached labor available	Family labor employed			Attached labor employed	Underemployment of family farm workers		Underemployment of attached wage farm workers	
	Total	Male	Female	Male	Total	Male	Female	Male	Total hours	As per cent of labor available	Total hours	As per cent of labor available
January	174,240	159,264	14,976	12,096	72,628	53,064	19,564	7,848	101,612	58.32	4,248	35.12
February	173,088	155,232	17,856	11,088	37,630	27,732	9,898	3,852	135,458	78.37	7,236	65.26
March	181,656	168,384	13,272	12,864	110,517	72,032	38,485	10,476	71,139	39.16	2,388	18.56
April	183,576	170,880	12,696	17,664	113,128	80,739	32,389	14,623	70,448	38.38	3,041	17.22
May	191,109	177,400	13,709	23,800	128,070	93,810	34,260	18,419	63,039	32.99	5,381	22.61
June	184,992	175,200	9,792	19,200	192,284	129,361	62,923	19,830	−7,292	−3.94	−630	−3.28
July	182,299	172,032	10,267	17,856	176,020	112,558	63,462	18,106	6,279	3.44	−250	−1.40
August	180,826	169,344	11,482	16,704	138,660	93,505	45,155	15,979	42,166	23.32	725	4.34
September	194,478	181,000	13,478	17,600	118,496	83,737	34,759	13,818	75,982	39.07	3,782	21.49
October	194,302	181,400	12,902	18,800	190,042	132,900	57,142	19,743	4,260	2.19	−943	−5.02
November	171,250	159,456	11,794	15,488	119,425	89,611	29,814	15,253	51,825	30.26	235	1.52
December	151,245	141,760	9,485	12,000	76,627	58,119	18,508	9,468	74,618	49.34	2,532	21.10
Total	2,163,061	2,011,352	151,709	195,160	1,473,527	1,027,168	446,359	167,415	689,534	31.88[b]	27,745	14.22[b]

[a] 60 farm districts, 582 farms.
[b] Based on yearly (total) figures.
SOURCE: Data for labor available are based on table 11. Labor employed figures are based on data provided by the Bank of Korea, Research Department.

CONCLUSION

The accuracy of our measurement of labor available and labor employed depends, of course, on the validity of assumptions as well as the representativeness of the sample. In our determination of labor available, the important assumptions are the exclusion of the inactive population; the allotment of 1.3 women for household duties; the 280 and 268 annual workdays figured for male and female workers, respectively; the estimate of eight work hours available per day; and the coefficients of labor available, 1.0 for the male farm worker from 15–59 years of age and 0.6 for the female worker in the same age range.

In considering the volume of labor employed, we set forth only one important assumption—that of its coefficient.

It should be pointed out that there may be a degree of error in all our assumptions and that to the extent of such possible error the calculations of idle labor we shall make in the next chapter may be inexact. Keeping in mind such possible minor deviations between reality and our assumptions, let us now look at our measurement of employment and underemployment in the Korean agricultural community.

V

Measurement of Underemployment

Technical and Tradition-directed

Table 12 (p. 76) shows the volume of underemployment, computed on the basis of labor available and labor employed, and figure 3 shows the extent of underemployment as given in table 12. The upper line indicates percentages of underemployment of self-supporting family farm labor; the lower line represents the underemployment of attached wage labor. Three conditions are apparent in the chart: (1) There is much seasonal variation in employment conditions in Korean agriculture. (2) There are shortages of family labor in peak agriculture seasons; in other words, there is no chronic underemployment, but only seasonal underemployment. (3) Self-supporting family workers are relatively more underemployed than attached wageworkers.

These conditions will be analyzed in detail to show the possible implications of each. To summarize briefly, our conclusions drawn from this inquiry are: (1) For Korean agriculture as a whole, approximately 30 per cent of the total labor time available (i.e., self-supporting family labor plus attached wage labor) is annually unutilized. (2) Disguised unemployment in the sense of chronic idle labor does not exist. (3) Approximately 62 per cent of the unutilized labor, or about 19 per cent of the total labor available, represents tradition-directed underemployment. This cannot be considered available for alternative use unless there are significant social changes and/or substantial additions of capital. (4) Technical underemployment, including both self-supporting family labor and wage labor, amounts to approximately 12 per cent of the total labor available, or about 38 per cent of the total unutilized labor. (5) The volume of tradition-directed underemployment is greater than the underemployment of self-supporting family labor stemming from the hiring of wage labor.

PRELIMINARY OBSERVATION
OF EMPLOYMENT CONDITIONS

Employment in the Korean agricultural community is classified by the Korean government into two major activities: "own farming" and "other farming," the latter meaning performing farm activities on other people's land or on community projects (see appendix table 1). Employment on one's own farm amounts to about 72 per cent of all hours spent in farm employment. Employment in other farming (performed by the members of the farm family, including attached laborers) amounts to approximately 28 per cent of total labor time.

Of the "own farming," cultivation of rice and summer grains (barley and wheat) is the most important single agricultural activity. Rice takes up about 23 per cent of the total number of hours spent in farm employment, the summer grains occupying about 10 per cent of the total labor time. Subsidiary occupations include animal husbandry (about 4.7 per cent), sericulture (about 0.5 per cent), and others such as grain refining, handicrafts, forestry, fishery, and commerce (about 18 per cent).

Wage labor, which is the largest single item in "other farming," about 9 per cent of the total employment, includes those workers who are hired out to earn wages in either farming or nonfarming, but excludes family members in salaried employment, such as teachers and clerical workers. Compulsory labor is work without remuneration imposed by the national and local governments, consisting of the construction or repairing of public utilities such as highways and bridges; it accounts for less than 0.9 per cent of the total labor employed. Other work includes building and

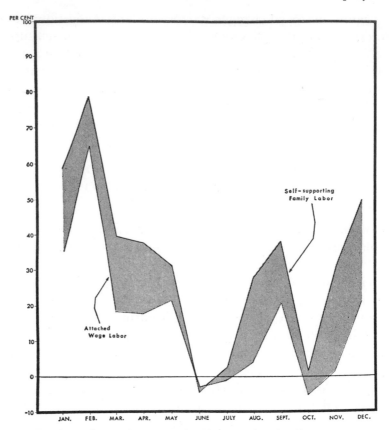

FIG. 3. Underemployment of self-supporting family workers
and attached wage laborers, Korea, 1959.

repairing of houses, fishing, gathering firewood, and voluntary
unpaid work for neighbors or for the community (18 per cent).

An understanding of these different categories of employment
will be very useful when we discuss the problem of underemployment in connection with so-called disguised unemployment. For
the conceptual analysis of underemployment, and for its correct
measurement, we must show within these categories their components of different sexes, age groups, and kinds of labor (i.e.,
self-supporting family labor and wage labor).

It may be useful, for the sake of clarity, to repeat here that,
according to the sample inquiry (see appendix table 2), farming

in Korea is carried out by three principal groups: self-supporting family labor, attached wage labor, and casual wage labor. Self-supporting family labor has two variants: the farm-owning family, and resident or nonresident relatives. The former owns the land and other farm property, whereas the latter share in the work and in the total output resulting from the joint labor, not as employees, but as members of the family. Attached workers are usually hired on a yearly basis. Casual workers are employed in busy seasons, primarily on a daily basis, when the family workers cannot handle all the work themselves. The classification of a person as a family worker does not necessarily imply a completely self-supporting status. A certain amount of family labor is hired out for wages. This is shown clearly in the "other farming" category in appendix table 1. Wage employment of family laborers is more prevalent among small-farm owners than among families owning relatively large farms.[1] Self-supporting family labor performs approximately 80 per cent of all the agricultural work done. Of this, about 70 per cent is done by male workers.[2]

Attached wageworkers put in a little less than 9 per cent of the total employment time. The amount of labor performed by casual workers accounts for a little more than 12 per cent of employment time. About one-fourth of this casual work is done by women. Therefore, attached labor and casual labor together account for about 21 per cent of the time spent in farm work (see appendix table 2).

A final point in this preliminary survey of the farm employment situation in Korea is the relative importance of work actually performed by different age groups. The active population carries out more than 95 per cent of the work done; the balance is done by the inactive population. Of the work done by the active population, women perform about 27 per cent. Of the work done by the inactive population, about 38 per cent is done by women.

---

[1] See Bank of Korea, Research Department, *Annual Economic Review*, 1959 (Seoul, 1959), sec. 1, p. 43.

[2] It must be noted in this connection that the 1.3 women allocated to household activity in our measurement of labor available need not, in reality, perform household duties exclusively, and likewise that the farm workers available, which we estimated with some care, need not specialize in farming only.

SEASONAL FLUCTUATIONS IN EMPLOYMENT

Underemployment in Korean agriculture is very severe in slack seasons. It is most pronounced in February; and there is much underemployment throughout the rest of the year except in the months of peak agricultural activity—June, July, and October.

These seasonal characteristics of Korean agriculture will make clearer the problem of underemployment. When spring comes, in March, winter crops and vegetables are growing rapidly and must receive adequate care. In late spring, some fields must be cleared, plowed, and fertilized for rice seedbeds. In late May the barley harvest begins, and work preparatory to rice transplanting absorbs much of the labor. Thus the extent of underemployment declines steadily from March on, and in June and July all the available workers are mobilized.

The general pattern of labor employed follows the pattern of labor engaged in rice cultivation. Rice cultivation takes up about 23 per cent of all farm time. The busiest months are June and July, when the rice is transplanted, and October, when it is harvested. It is in these months that the family farm workers alone cannot accomplish all the work. The cultivation of rice requires unusually intensive work—plowing, transplanting, and weeding—more work than for any other crop. The intensive plowing of watered, clay-loam soil, to allow for adequate percolation of air and water, is arduous and time-consuming. Moreover, a constant supply of water must be provided while the rice is ripening. When rain is insufficient, this is usually accomplished by hard labor, with simple facilities. Power-driven pumps are very rarely available to Korean farmers. When there is little or no rain, the farmers have no other choice but to wait for it. If excessive rain causes a flood that washes off the already transplanted rice, the farmers must later replant it.[3]

Although the cultivation of rice is the major agricultural activity influencing the volume of employment or underemploy-

---

[3] As insurance against this contingency, the farmers usually prepare more than the required amount of rice plants. The surplus rice plants are simply wasted if there is no flood.

ment on the Korean farm, there is, simultaneously, other work that must be done in the peak season. In June and July, the farmers are busy not only in paddy fields but also in dry fields, which constitute about 40 per cent of the total cultivated land. Various vegetables, fruits, and summer crops other than paddy rice must be produced by using the uplands, or dry fields. Transplanting and weeding are particularly time-consuming. Strenuous operations such as plowing and harrowing are usually done by men. But such strenuous work cannot be done continuously; therefore workers are either employed for a shorter day or transferred to lighter work for part of the same day. Light work such as animal husbandry, haymaking, and sparrow watching is often done by children. Other kinds of light work, such as sericulture, are usually assigned to women in the active age group, to children, or to older people.

When the peak summer agricultural season is over, much of the labor available retires from field work. Weeding, fertilizing, and harrowing are the chief agricultural tasks after the planting season. In August and September labor is very much underemployed. The rice is harvested in October. Family farm labor is supplemented at this time by some casual labor, together with help from inactive family members. When the rice harvest is over, the land must be cleared, plowed, and sown for winter barley.

Harvesting and threshing usually take from one-fifth to one-third of the labor time spent on a crop. Harvesting is done with no other equipment than a sickle. The machine thresher has been introduced—the sample survey shows that one of three farm households actually owns a thresher (see appendix table 3)—but the poor farmer must still use primitive methods. Harvesting is a rush job which has to be done within a comparatively limited period of time; consequently, a substantial amount of labor is hired for this operation. Transplanting and harvesting are the main agricultural operations in which women are employed.

The harvested crops are often carried on the men's backs, as draft animals are relatively scarce in Korean farming. In 1959 only 891,919 households of 2,267,419 owned cattle; only 12,420 farms raised horses; there were only 112 asses in all Korea.[4]

---

[4] Korea, Ministry of Agriculture and Forestry, *Year Book of Agriculture and Forestry*, 1960 (Seoul, 1960), pp. 2, 148–149.

Our sample inquiry shows that less than one of four farm households owns an ox for work in the fields, and the average number of carts owned by farm households is .08 (see appendix table 3).

Once the October work has been completed, farmers have a long recess. There is now a period of idleness, culminating at the end of February, when 78.37 per cent of the family labor available is without work. This lack of work in the winter months and in part of the summer growing season could be alleviated by increasing subsidiary farm employment such as domestic handicrafts, sericulture, dairy production, and animal husbandry, as well as by seasonal wage employment in rural or even in urban areas. Under the prevailing conditions, subsidiary work either at home or away from home is very limited. The winter months of November, December, January, and February account for most of the unutilized labor of Korean farm workers.

Employment opportunities in slack seasons, either in self-supporting or wage-paid labor, are very limited. Being poorly provided with resources and opportunities for work outside their own farms, most farmers remain very much underemployed. They are occupied in slack seasons only by a limited number of tasks, such as roofing houses, gathering firewood, looking after the animals, making straw ropes and mats, and selling crops or vegetables in the nearby market. All these activities are sporadic. Thus many farmers are mostly idle in slack seasons. After the completion of the rice harvest, fields must be cleared and plowed for winter barley; once the barley has been sown, farmers go into a long retirement from active field work until the next barley harvest in May. The important conclusion is that, because of the seasonal variation of agricultural activities and the limited alternative employment opportunities, the Korean agricultural community is characterized by tremendous seasonal underemployment and a relatively high labor requirement in peak seasons.

SIGNIFICANCE OF THE DIFFERENCE BETWEEN CASUAL WAGE LABOR AND ATTACHED WAGE LABOR

Labor shortage in peak seasons is a major problem,[5] which must be solved either by hiring extra labor and using inactive family members, or by introducing laborsaving devices. As the work that can be done by the inactive population is minor, the only way to solve the problem, given the constraint of the *ceteris paribus* assumption, is to hire casual wage labor. There are two variants of casual labor: the labor hired by the sample family, and the wage labor performed by the sample family. Both help to fill the labor shortage in busy seasons. This condition prevails even on very small farms. It is important to realize, in defining agricultural wage labor, that casual labor is mainly performed by self-supporting family workers, hired by neighboring farmers only occasionally and so intermittently that each individual casual laborer, although he receives a wage of some kind, works so few days a year that he cannot be considered a bona fide wage laborer. On the other hand, although those whom we regard as attached agricultural wage laborers are relatively few in number, each individual works at least one-half of his total employment time (i.e., at least one-half of the standard 280 days a year). Nonattached agricultural wage labor is practically nonexistent in Korea. We might say, in passing, that this condition does not apply to all underdeveloped agricultural countries.[6]

---

[5] In this connection it is worth commenting on Rosenstein-Rodan's concept of disguised unemployment. He says it exists when labor is chronically unemployed and underemployed. In other words, he claims that even in a period of peak labor employment there is still a balance of unused available labor; this is the significance of his term "chronically." In Korea there is no chronic agricultural unemployment. For the measurement of disguised unemployment in a chronic sense, cf. P. N. Rosenstein-Rodan, "Disguised Unemployment and Underemployment in Agriculture," *Monthly Bulletin of Agricultural Economics and Statistics*, VI (July-Aug., 1957), 1–7.

[6] Agricultural wage laborers in India make up more than 32 per cent of the total farm work force. Of these, more than 90 per cent are casual nonattached laborers, and the rest are attached wage laborers (India, Ministry of Labour, *Agricultural Labour Enquiry: Report on Intensive Survey of Agricultural Labour*, I [Delhi, 1955], 37–44). In Korean agriculture, family workers are those who work mostly on their own account, and only attached workers who labor primarily for wages are significant as agricultural laborers. Agricultural labor, or attached wage labor, will be referred to hereafter as wage labor.

DIFFERENCES IN UNDEREMPLOYMENT
OF SELF-SUPPORTING FAMILY LABOR
AND ATTACHED WAGE LABOR

In rural Korea, traditional social institutions such as the extended-family system and the clan system constitute an important part of the people's value system. The existence of these social institutions tends to involve more relatives in farm work than would otherwise be the case; this causes increased underemployment among self-supporting farm labor. Attached wageworkers who do not own land and have no alternative employment opportunities usually secure farm employment as attached workers.

Within the Korean agricultural community, the average per capita income even of self-supporting farm families that own relatively large holdings is not much higher than the biological minimum. The larger the holding, the larger the number of nonfarm-owning family members; and most attached labor is hired on the largest farms (i.e., farms of 4.9 acres or more). The average annual income per member in these families is about 94,000 *hwan,* including "donations" and government subsidies of about 7,200 *hwan.*[7] The average per capita annual income of these families is higher by about 23,000 *hwan* (or about 23 U.S. dollars) than the average yearly wage income of attached laborers. Because the earning level of self-supporting family workers is so low and there is considerable underemployment among them, it is hard to understand why, from a purely economic point of view, they retain nonfarm-owning family labor and attached wageworkers instead of dismissing them, which would improve their own economic condition.

Underemployment of self-supporting family workers, for 1959, amounted to 31.88 per cent of their labor time available. Monthly conditions varied from a labor shortage in June of about 4 per cent of the self-supporting family labor available, and a negligible amount of underemployment in July and October, to underemployment of 78.37 per cent in February. The extent of underem-

---

[7] See table 19 in chap. viii.

ployment of attached wageworkers, for 1959, amounted to 14.22 per cent of their labor time available. For them, monthly conditions ranged from a labor shortage in June, July, and October to underemployment of 65.26 per cent in February. The difference in the extent of underemployment between self-supporting family workers and attached wageworkers was substantial, with the former experiencing greater underemployment.

The above information shows that a certain number of attached wage laborers are hired, even though the employers themselves—farm-owning family workers—may be underemployed at the same time. Nevertheless, the wageworker is also very much underemployed, although, collectively, wage labor experiences less underemployment than self-supporting family workers. This phenomenon is of particular social and economic significance in the Koreans employment situation; it emphasizes the importance of the distinction between wage labor and self-supporting family labor. It points up the necessity for a breakdown of the traditional institutions that perpetuate this impractical employment situation.

It must be stressed, however, that the social ramifications of this employment situation serve only as necessary, not sufficient, criteria for measuring technical and tradition-directed underemployment. So far, none of the factors in our analysis—the amount of attached wage labor hired by the self-supporting family, the amount of underemployment of the family members, the difference in the extent of underemployment between wage labor and family labor—is a sufficient basis for accurate measurement of these two types of underemployment. What other criteria are needed?

MEASUREMENT OF TECHNICAL
AND TRADITION-DIRECTED UNDEREMPLOYMENT

Keeping the foregoing contentions in mind, let us proceed to find additional criteria for measuring underemployment. Our study of the Korean agricultural community is not based on direct personal investigation of its behavior. Rather, it is based on certain valid assumptions, or objective criteria, developed as a result of careful observation of the technical and social characteristics of that community.

We assume that currently attached wageworkers, as a whole, are utilized as fully as possible, except for some inevitable idleness in off seasons; that they are socially marginal individuals; and that the idleness of this class of workers may be considered true surplus labor. We then proceed to postulate a hypothetical situation where no traditional social institutions exist in this society —a relaxation of the *ceteris paribus* assumption only for the purpose of analysis. This conjecture leads to a situation in which even family workers not uprooted as a result of this social change would also become socially marginal individuals, for there would be no traditions to which to cling. Then each one of the family workers remaining on the land would be employed only to the same extent as the attached wage laborer was employed (and underemployed) before the hypothetical social change.

As these assumptions are crucial, they will be explained in detail. It is necessary first, however, to be more specific about our method. When these assumptions hold, a simple equation leads to the estimate of current magnitude of the two types of underemployment under discussion: tradition-directed underemployment equals labor available minus labor not uprooted. The formula that measures the labor not uprooted (i.e., labor remaining in a given rural area after the hypothetical social change) is: $a = \dfrac{\text{TLE}}{r}$, where TLE is total labor employed (in terms of hours); r indicates the proportion of attached-wage-labor employment in the actual (not the hypothetical) situation, in relation to an optimum which is full employment; and a indicates the amount of labor not uprooted as a result of the hypothetical social change.

Thus, $a = \dfrac{\text{TLE}}{r}$ is the total labor time required after the social change, and it includes the total amount of labor employed actually (not after the hypothetical change) plus the actual (in the above sense of not hypothetical) technical underemployment. This assumes that family workers not uprooted by the hypothetical social change would be technically underemployed to the same extent as wage laborers are underemployed in the real (not conjectured) situation. The amount of technical underemployment is then $a(1-r)$, where $1-r$ is technical underemployment as a proportion of labor required after the social change.

The actual (in the sense of existing within the present *status quo*) volume of tradition-directed underemployment is equal to the amount of labor that could be displaced through the breakdown of social institutions. It is measured by the fomula, $TDU = TLA - \dfrac{TLE}{r}$, where TLA is total labor available, and TDU represents actual tradition-directed underemployment (before the social change). In other words, the formula shows that tradition-directed underemployment equals total labor available minus the total of labor employed and technical underemployment, all in terms of labor-hours. The formula for tradition-directed underemployment, in proportion to total labor available, may be expressed as $1 - \dfrac{TLE}{TLA \times r}$.

Technical underemployment and tradition-directed underemployment, computed on the basis of the above equations, are shown in table 13. On a yearly average computation, they amount, respectively, to about 11.58 per cent and 18.83 per cent of the total labor time available. The relative proportion of these two types of underemployment to total underemployment is about 38 per cent and 62 per cent, respectively.

The percentages of underemployment cited above are based on the concept of "labor available" which differs from the traditional concept of "labor force." Labor force may be thought of as being equivalent to that amount of manpower which excludes tradition-directed idle labor. According to this definition of labor force, approximately 15 per cent of the manpower in Korean agriculture is not utilized, representing technical idle labor.

VALIDITY OF THE ASSUMPTIONS

To obtain criteria upon which the assumptions rest, further investigation was made of the labor structure and the pattern of employment shaped by technical and social environments.

Although the attached wage laborer in the Korean rural com-

TABLE 13

TECHNICAL AND TRADITION-DIRECTED UNDEREMPLOYMENT EXPRESSED IN MAN-HOUR EQUIVALENT, KOREA,[a] 1959

Month	Total labor (family and wage) available (TLA)	Total labor (family and wage) employed (TLE)	Total (family and wage) underemployment	Total (family and wage) underemployment as percentage of TLA	Rates of employment of attached farm wage workers (r)[b]	$\frac{TLE}{r}$ (amount of labor required)[c]	$\frac{TLE}{r}$ − TLE (technical underemployment)[d]	Technical underemployment as percentage of TLA	TLA − $\frac{TLE}{r}$ (tradition-directed underemployment)[e]	Tradition-directed underemployment as percentage of TLA
January	186,336	80,476	105,860	56.81	0.6488	124,038	43,562	23.38	62,298	33.43
February	184,176	41,482	142,694	77.48	0.3474	119,407	77,925	42.31	64,769	35.17
March	194,520	120,993	73,527	37.80	0.8144	148,567	27,574	14.18	45,953	23.62
April	201,240	127,751	73,489	36.52	0.8278	154,326	26,575	13.21	46,914	23.31
May	214,909	146,489	68,420	31.84	0.7739	189,287	42,798	19.91	25,622	11.92
June	204,192	212,114	−7,922	—	1.0328	204,192	—	—	—	—
July	200,155	194,126	6,029	3.01	1.0140	200,155	6,029	3.01	—	—
August	197,530	154,639	42,891	21.71	0.9566	161,654	7,016	3.55	35,875	18.16
September	212,078	132,314	79,764	37.61	0.7851	168,531	36,217	17.08	43,547	20.53
October	213,102	209,785	3,317	1.56	1.0501	213,102	3,317	1.56	—	—
November	186,738	134,678	52,060	27.88	0.9848	136,757	2,079	1.11	49,981	26.77
December	163,245	86,095	77,150	47.26	0.7890	109,119	23,024	14.14	54,126	33.16
Total	2,358,221	1,640,942	717,279	30.42[f]	0.8573[f]	1,914,081[f]	273,139[f]	11.58[f]	444,140[f]	18.83[f]

[a] 60 farm districts.
[b] The letter "r" represents the ratio of total hours of employment of the attached wageworker to total hours of labor available of the attached wageworker.
[c] The amount of labor required is equivalent to the amount of the remaining labor as a result of the social change. The amount of the remaining labor in June, July, and October is assumed to be the same as the labor available in the respective month.
[d] Technical underemployment equals seasonal underemployment.
[e] Tradition-directed underemployment corresponds to the amount of labor displaced as a consequence of the social change.
[f] Based on yearly (total) figure. Because of the assumption of labor remaining in June, July, and October, monthly figures are not applicable.
SOURCE: Based on table 11.

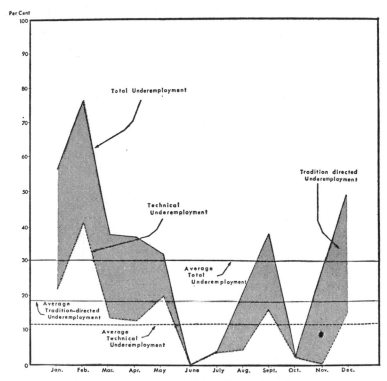

Fig. 4. Total, technical, and tradition-directed underemployment as percentages of total labor available (60 farm districts, Korea, 1959).

munity is involved in the total value system, he cannot be thought of as being idle in a tradition-directed sense. In the agricultural community, one who has little or no land to cultivate and no possibility of finding alternative employment usually becomes an attached wageworker. The average attached worker's income in 1959 was about 71,000 *hwan* (about 71 U.S. dollars), which included various allowances in kind, as well as wages in cash. Thus the attached wageworker barely earns the minimum necessary for his own survival, leaving virtually nothing for a family. From this standpoint he is not able to support a family; he remains unmarried. He can be said to belong, as a result, to a social class that may indeed be termed a lonely crowd, in a literal sense. As he cannot rely on the income of his parents (assuming that he still has them), work is an absolute necessity for his survival. Furthermore, as a wageworker he is hardly a part of the firmly tradition-directed segment of the society in which he exists. He is, in this sense, an economically and socially marginal individual. From the standpoint of the farm owner also, the underemployment of the attached wage laborer in his household must be looked upon as technical underemployment, as his employer can do nothing to give him more work. Although the wage laborer is a hired worker and works as much as circumstances allow, he is left underemployed in most of the off seasons. Given the constraint of fixed technical means of production and the institution of attached labor, the farm owner can do little about the seasonal underemployment of hired labor.

This leads us to the conclusion that the extent of employment or underemployment of attached wageworkers may safely be used as a yardstick to measure the magnitude of tradition-directed and technical underemployment. Expressed in another way, the pattern of employment of attached wage laborers may be regarded as a basic indicator of the amount of labor required, *ceteris paribus,* in Korean agriculture, which includes seasonal technical underemployment. However, as a safeguard against possible unwarranted inferences being drawn from the above conclusion, a few remarks may be in order.

My argument is not simply, as is believed by some, that when a farm household hires wage labor, only unutilized self-supporting family labor, corresponding to the amount of wage labor hired, would constitute tradition-directed underemployment. If one follows this view, the amount of tradition-directed underemployment is simply the same as that of the wage labor hired by the self-supporting family labor. If this were so, then my point of view would be no better than a straight forward and naïve application of "profit maximization," which requires no more than a single page for argument. Also, if tradition-directed underemployment is regarded as only that part of underemployment of self-supporting family labor which derives from the substitution of wage labor for its own labor, tradition-directed underemployment would be only about 8 per cent and technical underemployment would be about 22 per cent of the total labor available. It is hardly believable that, *ceteris paribus,* removable labor in this economy would be as high as 22 per cent of the total labor available. A full understanding of the meaning of my assumption is crucial at this point in order to grasp the rationale of my method of estimating underemployment.

The self-supporting family workers, after the hypothetical social change, would be situated, in regard to employment, as the attached wageworkers are in the actual situation. This means that they would be employed to approximately the same extent as the attached wage laborers are employed in the real situation. It also means that all the underemployment, after the social change, would be technical and none would be tradition-directed because, hypothetically, the traditions would no longer obtain. Tradition-directed idle labor has meaning only in the milieu as it was before the conjectured social change; it is measured here by the estimated amount of displaced labor resulting from the social change.

The hypothetical breakdown of institutions would uproot not only attached wage labor but also some of the nonfarm-owning family labor—the farm owner's relatives. The extent of the uprooting of this category of workers would be commensurate with the amount of work actually available. Therefore, the amount of tradition-directed underemployment would not necessarily be equal to the amount of attached wage labor in the real situation, as the extent of the uprooting of nonfarm-owning family members would be an added factor in calculating underemployment of the tradition-directed type.

On the other hand, I do not believe that, when a farm household hires attached wageworkers, all the unutilized self-supporting family labor must be considered tradition-directed underemployment. Even if the self-supporting family workers were willing to work to the extent of the attached wageworkers, they could not always do so because there is only so much work to go around. Because of this, even if the assumption is reasonable that wage laborers as a whole are not underemployed in a tradition-directed sense, we cannot conclude that the difference between a wage laborer's underemployment and that of the self-supporting family worker (see figure 3) is a sufficient measure of tradition-directed underemployment of self-supporting family labor. In the hypothetical situation, a sufficient amount of labor must be displaced from the self-supporting status in order for the remaining family laborers to work as much as the attached wageworkers and the nonland-owning relatives in the real situation.

From the formula $\dfrac{TLE}{r}$, it may be deduced that the absolute amount of technical underemployment increases as the total labor employed increases; it increases at the rate (r) of the underemployment of attached wageworkers. The rationale for this rigid variation may be explained by two factors: the employment situation of attached wageworkers, and the seasonal fluctuation in labor demand. Once we admit that attached wageworkers as a whole are as fully utilized as possible, the amount of labor actually required depends on the seasonal variations of labor demand. As we observed before, it is typical of underdeveloped agricultural economies that the greater the labor demand in peak agricultural seasons, the more labor is unutilized in off seasons. In a country like Korea, where an undiversified agriculture prevails, the above pattern of underemployment is quite obvious. This seasonal variation of labor demand is expressed in the formula $\dfrac{TLE}{r}$, in order to estimate the total labor required (or the potential amount of labor which should remain in the farm household after the hypothetical social change). More explicitly, the formula may be read as the potential amount of labor required (i.e., a) to carry out the total work (i.e., TLE) when the role of the attached wageworker is taken over by the remaining agricultural labor (i.e., the farm-owning labor) after the social change.

The above reasoning is valid only when the attached wageworkers, whom we have been using as a yardstick, are as fully employed as possible. Of course, normally, in the rigid relationship of employer-employee, in Korea as well as elsewhere, they are as fully employed as possible.

Thus we use the formula $\dfrac{TLE}{r}$ to measure the amount of labor required after the conjectured social change. More specifically, the extent of employment of attached wage labor may be regarded as a basic indicator of the amount of labor empirically (apart from tradition-directed attitudes) required in Korean agriculture. The amount of labor that would be displaced by the hypothetical social change, or the current tradition-directed underemployment, is thus measured by subtracting the amount of labor actually necessary or required from the total labor time actually (in the real situation) available for Korean farming. This is the rationale of our assumptions.

CONCLUSION

What policy implications may be drawn from this distinction between the two types of underemployment? The answer is that technical (open) underemployment alone is true surplus labor, the only withdrawable surplus labor under the *ceteris paribus* assumption. Given the constraint of this assumption, tradition-directed (closed) underemployment cannot be withdrawn from the land unless, of course, a totalitarian method is adopted.[8] Hence the supply of labor in these underdeveloped agricultural economies is not unlimited,[9] as has been suggested by W. A. Lewis; and all the unemployed in tradition-directed societies are not surplus labor, as David Riesman seems to suggest.[10]

It is relevant and it will, we hope, help to clarify the scope of our study to say here, in retrospect, that, as the traditional concept of disguised unemployment is inadequate to explain the true extent of surplus labor in underdeveloped countries, we have not attempted to measure the surplus labor that is supposed to exist (in a "hidden" or "disguised" form) among employed farm labor. Instead, we measured two components of unutilized labor—technical (open) and tradition-directed (closed) underemployment— by comparing the hours of work available for farming and the hours of work actually used in farming (both were converted into man-hour equivalents by using coefficients of labor available and labor employed). The underemployment we measured is all visi-

---

[8] The Nurkse scheme is a compulsory method (Ragnar Nurkse, *Problems of Capital Formation in Underdeveloped Countries* [Oxford: Basil Blackwell, 1955], p. 37).

[9] Cf. W. A. Lewis, "Economic Development with Unlimited Supplies of Labour," *Manchester School of Economic and Social Studies*, XXII (May, 1954), 148–151, and "Unlimited Labour: Further Notes," *Manchester School of Economic and Social Studies*, XXVI (Jan., 1958), 2–3.

[10] David Riesman *et al.*, *The Lonely Crowd: A Study of the Changing American Character* (New Haven: Yale University Press, 1950), p. 12.

ble, not disguised, in the sense of the traditional school. The traditional school views all farm workers as actually working, and asserts the marginal productivity of employed workers over a wide range to be zero. But our actual investigation of Korean farming shows that the line between working and not working can be clearly drawn: farmers are not "wasting their time" while they are working; they are in fact working at their physical limit in order to get the work done as fast as possible. It seems to me that there is little sense in attempting to measure the surplus labor of farm workers who are actually working.

Technical underemployment has nothing disguised or hidden about it. Where tradition-directed underemployment is concerned, however, there is something there which draws a veil over it. It follows, therefore, that if the term "disguised" has any meaning, it is this tradition-directed employment which is, in a sense, "disguised."

It seems appropriate here to concretize our notion of a hypothetical social change. A sudden breakdown of prevailing social institutions is an important conjecture in this study; the assumption is made, of course, for purely analytical purposes. This hypothetical revolution in social institutions conjectures what would stimulate economic motivation in comparison with the noneconomic values prevailing in existing rural life, values that are the cornerstones of tradition-directed underemployment.

Perhaps our analysis should not stop here: What would the situation be if the hypothetical social change actually materialized? Would the people uprooted as a result of the change—the tradition-directed underemployed—be usable surplus labor within the existing political system? The social institutions and the value system of the rural Korean community contribute significantly to political stability. Were the social changes we postulate to materialize, with their consequent large-scale technical unemployment, the uprooted, unemployed people would seek some kind of political solution to their economic plight. In other words, deep social unrest would result unless remedies were quickly offered. Such remedies would require vast sums of capital investment. We must emphasize here that the eventuality of such social unrest is not within the scope of our conjectured social change; it contemplates only social, not political, ramifications. Our hypothetical social change does violate the assumption of *ceteris paribus,* but only for purpose of estimating, through analysis, the volume of tradition-directed underemployment. After we arrive at this measure, our discussion returns to its former assumption of *ceteris paribus.*

VI

Socioeconomic Aspects of the Korean Agricultural Community

Economic policy to help solve the problem of underemployment in underdeveloped rural areas may be directed toward increasing employment within the agricultural community itself, or it may attempt to remove labor from the land. In this chapter we shall analyze the former approach; consideration of the latter method is deferred to the following chapter.

The Korean agricultural economy is essentially static, in that, under the prevailing social and economic conditions, there is little room for change without substantial capital investment. But capital is chronically very scarce. In order to get free of the static condition and initiate economic development, the agricultural community must break through its old social institutions. It is for this reason that we start our search for a solution to the problem of underemployment with a discussion of the main characteristics of social institutions in rural Korea.

THE TRADITIONAL KOREAN SOCIAL ORGANIZATION IN RURAL AREAS

The key to rural social organization is the existence of close family ties among the people, in the clan, and in village life. The family system represents an adoption of Chinese customs based on Confucian principles. It is the duty of older members of a family to care for younger members. The younger members, in turn, when they become adults, have the obligation of caring for the elderly. Filial duty is regarded as the highest virtue in Korean social culture. The institution of polygamy, with its proliferation of offspring, still prevails. The clan system, with its wide inclusion of distant relatives, is also an important feature of Korean social organization; a number of families within a rural village are often grouped together, in part because of proximity, into clans. Shannon McCune's description of the Korean family system stresses further details:

> The usual pattern of family life is founded on the Confucian concept of the correct relationship between people—the "five relationships." These revolve about the ideas of superiority and inferiority: thus, the wife is subordinate to the husband, the sons to the father, the younger brother to the older brother, the younger friend to the older friend, and finally the subject to the ruler. Hence the senior male member, usually the father and husband, holds the ruling position in the group. . . .
>
> The Korean village family unit very often occupies a single household. The sons' wives, who are from another clan, become a part of the family unit, and achieve something more than inferior status only if they give birth to males who will carry on the family line. A mother who has had sons—and ultimately grandsons—is able to exert strong behind-the-scene influence, which may be exercised indirectly through the daughters-in-law or through the father and husband. . . .
>
> Within the village is an informal structure designed to benefit the allied families. The heads of the families act as leaders of the village. . . . These persons are called upon to arbitrate disputes, keep peace and order, stimulate public works, and act as liaison for higher political authorities.[1]

Farmhouses cluster at the foot of hills or on their easy slopes, accessible to the farm land located in the valley. This type of vil-

---

[1] Shannon McCune, *Korea's Heritage: A Regional and Social Geography* (Rutland, Vt., and Tokyo: Charles E. Tuttle Co., 1956), pp. 72–73. For detailed information on Korean village life see Eisuke Zensho, *Sei-Katsu, Cho-Tai Cho-Sa* [*Living Conditions Inquiry*], Chosa Siryo, nos. 28–29, 32, 38–39, 40–41 (Seoul: Chosen-So-Tokoo-Hoo [Chosen Publishing Co.], 1931, 1933, 1934, 1935).

lage life permits the farmers to arrange and organize group work when necessary:

This group work seems to be a matter of great antiquity, though it is seldom found in Japan or in China, where most of the farm work is done by the farmer himself independently or with the members of his family only. It has the advantage that it promotes affinity among the members of a rural community, develops the cooperative spirit, diminishes the fatigue and weariness of working alone, and results in an increased efficiency of labor.[2]

The organization of group work is based on the principle of reciprocity.[3] Most of the mutual aid is given in peak agricultural seasons.

In general, for the rest of the year, farming is done mostly by family members and attached wageworkers. Nonfarm-owning family members are satisfied with such reward as is traditionally regarded as fair for their volunteered services rendered as members of the family, not as employees. The strong family ties, the clan, and the village system represent special values for those who live in a rural community. They enjoy a sense of "belonging" and of employment security through their family ties. This is why so many Koreans want to live in rural areas. Their preference is totally rational, rather than irrational.

AGRICULTURAL ORGANIZATION AND METHODS

Agricultural organization in Korea is closely related to the basic social system. When the son of a farm family sets up his own home, he is usually given a share of the family land. The land is split up in this way into increasingly smaller units with each generation. The absence of the law of primogeniture is one of the major reasons for the fragmentation of landholdings. Not only are the farms themselves small, but their areas are not contiguous, because each holding is subdivided into many tiny scattered plots, so that the farmer has to get from one to the other in the course of his daily work, with a substantial loss of time and energy.

It is generally believed that the smallness of the holdings not

---

[2] Hoon Koo Lee, *Land Utilization and Rural Economy in Korea* (Chicago: University of Chicago Press, 1936), p. 98.

[3] *Ibid.*, pp. 97–98.

only lessens the incentive to spend money on the maintenance of proper drains and embankments to prevent waterlogging and soil erosion, but also makes mechanization undesirable, and leads to a considerable "waste" of labor and land.[4] Unless drastic changes are made, however, these conditions will continue to prevail. As the reader will recall, such changes are not permissible in our framework of thinking: given the assumption of *ceteris paribus,* little could be done to change the prevailing conditions. Given the existing agricultural organization, the shape of technology, and the paucity of capital, labor that seems to be wasted is not really wasted if there is to be any production at all.

Lee's investigation shows that, on the average, each Korean farm household cultivates 4.3 land lots, which are at an average distance of about 1,000 feet from the farmstead. Of all the farms investigated (1,249 units), only one farmhouse was located right on the farm land, with no other lots to manage. Lots averaged 1 acre in size.[5] When there are paddy fields, the lots are further subdivided into many plots by solid, irregular, and permanent ridges. An agricultural economist describes the problem of fragmentation as follows: "Fragmentation is a dreadful example of want of rationalization in farming. Hundreds of thousands of miles are walked unnecessarily each year in peasant farming throughout the world." [6] Again, *ceteris paribus,* this walking is inevitable rather than unnecessary, if production is to go on at all. Korean farmers are well aware of the inconveniences and the disadvantages of fragmented, scattered small holdings. Proposals for consolidation, however, would encounter many objections on social, economic, and technical grounds.

Experience in other countries has shown that consolidation through mutual agreement is very difficult and involves heavy expenses. In France, Germany, Switzerland, Denmark, and Japan

[4] Kalka P. Bhatnagar *et al., Indian Rural Economy* (Parade-Kanpur: Kishore Publishing House, 1955), pp. 115–116.

[5] Lee, *op. cit.,* p. 98. For European examples see P. Lamartine Yates and D. Warriner, *Food and Farming in Post-War Europe* (London: Oxford University Press, 1943), p. 98.

[6] Louise E. Howard, *Labour in Agriculture: An International Survey* (London: Oxford University Press, 1935), p. 238. Other striking examples are shown in "Reconsolidation of Holdings in Germany," *International Labour Review,* XXV (May, 1932), 678–680, and Radhakamal Mukerjee, *The Rural Economy of India* (London: Longmans, Green, 1926), p. 33. For Japan, see Shiroshi Nasu, *Land Utilization in Japan* (Chicago: University of Chicago Press, 1929), p. 81.

the diversity and the insecurity of tenure, tenancy rights, and the illiteracy and backwardness of the cultivators were all deterrents to voluntary consolidation.[7] In Madras, India, the government encouraged voluntary consolidation in 1947–1948, but abandoned the experiment because consolidation proved ineffective while fragmentation (through inheritance, etc.) continued.[8] Moreover, consolidation of terraced paddy fields is technically difficult, as small sections are necessary in order to ensure that the water is of equal depth at all points.

Unless farmhouses were built in the fields, consolidation of holdings would bring the farmers no nearer to their land. As there are no safeguards against the frequent floods that barely miss the farmhouses clustered on the hillsides, it would be impractical to locate farmhouses right in the fields. On the positive side, the arrangement of the village and the layout of the fields give the cultivator a good diversity of crops, thereby ensuring continuity of food supply and protection against possible starvation. Land for paddy fields near ponds or wells is limited, so that a typical holding in a village consists of one plot of lowland with water supplied directly from the reservoir when rain is insufficient, and another on the hillside which is safe from floods. Between these two extremes lies higher land which can be used either as dry field or paddy field, and where crops other than rice can be grown. This distribution of holdings provides a diversity of output and affords some continuity of employment. Many of the advocates of consolidation fail to understand adequately the ecological conditions that have forced on the farmer the scattering of his landholdings. Indian agriculture in a typical rice tract seems to suffer from the same conditions:

. . . so long as dependence on the annual rainfall does not decrease, consolidation is a doubtful measure in India. Hailey rightly observes: "The whole agricultural system of the provinces has in fact been adopted to meet the predominant feature of the climatic conditions, *viz.*, the uncertainty of the rainfall. This has led the agriculturalist to aim at security rather than high results, and to frame his annual crop programme so as to eliminate the chances of total failure. This attitude may be seen in every phase of his operations—in the growing

---

[7] Bhatnagar *et al.*, *op. cit.*, p. 118.
[8] *Ibid.*, p. 119.

of two crops, often to the detriment of the main crop—in the habit of sowing mixed crops to the despair of the statistician—in his preference for hardy, if low-yielding varieties and, in the land system, in the distribution of the different classes of land so as to secure at least one crop in the year. It is not conducive to good agriculture, but it has enabled a dense population to meet with success the vicissitudes of the season." [9]

Rice is the most important crop in Korean agriculture. About 59 per cent of the total cultivated land is given over to rice paddy fields, and this rice constitutes about 56 per cent of the value of crop proceeds, or 49 per cent of the total average farm output. Labor employed in rice cultivation, nevertheless, is only 23 per cent of the total labor applied to all agricultural activities. It is therefore not an exaggeration to say that Korean agriculture can best be understood through consideration of its rice cultivation. The smallness of farms, and the establishing of village communities, are both connected with rice cultivation, which necessitates the breaking up of land into small plots surrounded by dikes, and the collective management of irrigation.

Korea, like other Asian nations, selected the crop that permitted it to make the most of the heavy rains which fall directly on the fields and, in addition, to profit from the enormous volume of the runoff from adjacent uncultivable mountain country. Throughout Asia, farmers have "adapted conditions to crops and crops to conditions until in rice they have a cereal which permits the most intense fertilization and at the same time the insuring of maximum yields against both drought and flood for dense populations." [10] Mukerjee gives a detailed account of this phenomenon:

Rice, which gives a maximum yield, is a good staple crop for dense populations. Where the population is not dense, however, it cannot be grown; for the cultivation of rice demands a large number of unskilled hands and arduous hand labour over relatively brief agricultural seasons. With a cheap supply of agricultural labour, little manure and with imperfect tools and implements, rice feeds large masses of population. Social cohesiveness among rice-growing peoples naturally is encouraged when a large population is concentrated in small fertile areas, while the flooding of the rice-fields during transplantation de-

[9] Mukerjee, *op. cit.*, p. 33.
[10] *Ibid.*, p. 20.

velops communal habits of agriculture and communal control of irrigation. It is this social cohesiveness which has governed the characteristic distribution of fields in China, Japan and India.

. . . the people with rare wisdom have combined both irrigation and
dry farming methods to an extent and with an intensity far beyond
anything the Western peoples have ever dreamed, to the end that
they might maintain their dense populations.[11]

Economists have also disagreed on the optimum farm size. It
has frequently been charged that the post–World War II land
reform in Korea,[12] which created a larger number of small farms
by breaking up large holdings, has not contributed to improvement in the methods of production and thus has not increased the

---

[11] *Ibid.*, pp. 20–21.

[12] The land reform in Korea was carried out in two stages: one by the United
States Military Government in Korea and the other by the Republic of Korea. In
1948 the U.S. Military Government sold 555,000 acres of previously Japanese-owned
land to 500,000 tenants (with a maximum holding of 4.90 acres permitted), in return
for a payment in kind, spread over fifteen years, equal to three times the annual
production of the principal crop on the land received.

The land reform law passed in 1950 by the Korean government concerned the
redistribution of some of the privately owned large estates. Its major provisions
were: (1) The government was to purchase all farm land not being tilled by the
owner and all land in excess of 7.35 acres, even if tilled by the owner. (2) The
compensation to the landowner was at the rate of 150 per cent of the average
annual yield. The principle of progressive diminution was to be applied: the larger
the area owned by one family, the lower the rate of compensation to be paid for
the land. (3) The land so purchased by the government (with bonds) was to be
resold at the same price to farmers to till. The order of priority was to be: the present
tillers (tenant farmers); farmers capable of cultivating more land than they already
possessed; war veterans' families if they had experience in farming; agricultural
laborers; and farm families repatriated from foreign countries. By the end of 1958,
952,731 households had received land from the distribution of privately owned land,
and 596,801 households had acquired property previously owned by Japanese. All in
all, 1,549,532 households (of the total of 2,218,323 farm households) were affected
by the land reform.

Of Korea's 4,869,871 cultivated acres, 1,128,048 were redistributed (about 23 per
cent). This figure would have been higher had it not been for voluntary sales by
landowners before the first stage of land reform. The land reforms in Korea have
been said to be unsuccessful in achieving some of their aims, such as elimination of
tenant farming and improvement of small peasants' living standards. Many farmers
had to revert to their former tenancy status because they could not meet the
payments for the land they received, owing to the lack of surplus product after
their own consumption.

Cf. Sidney Klein, *The Pattern of Land Tenure Reform in East Asia after World
War II* (New York: Bookman Associates, 1958), pp. 83–104; George M. McCune,
Korea Today (Cambridge: Harvard University Press, 1950), pp. 129–130; U.S. Department of State, Economic Commission, *Land Reform in Korea* (Seoul, 1947), p.
1; Korean Reconstruction Bank, *Economic Review*, 1945–1955 (Seoul, 1955), p. 44;
and Bank of Korea, Research Department, *Annual Economic Review*, 1959 (Seoul,
1959), sec. 1, p. 44.

volume of employment and income.[13] The object of land reform in Korea, as in other Asian countries such as Japan and Formosa, was the breaking up of the already scattered and fragmented large estates into small holdings. It did not seek to contribute to changes in the method and the organization of production. Rather, "the redistribution of land ownership seems to have been the sole achievement of the land tenure system." [14] Landlords in Korea, before the land reforms, had done no more than simply rent out land. They had been neither agricultural innovators nor suppliers of capital to their tenants; nor had they determined what crops were to be cultivated. They were "rentiers pure and simple." [15] This is why the redistribution of land is believed to have caused no change in the methods of production, progressive or regressive. A United Nations study emphasizes this point:

The land reforms in Asia are concerned primarily with the breaking up of great estates, which are large properties worked by small tenant-cultivators, and not large centrally managed enterprises as they are in Europe and in Latin America. The redistribution of land ownership can be carried through without involving any change in methods of production or any change in the scale of operation. The new legislation is enforcing measures for redistribution of income, not for the reorganization of production. It is not likely, therefore, to have harmful effects though the disruption of existing units of production, as might be the case if the sub-division of large and highly centralized farm units were in question. Since the scale of operation is in any case small, and since the landowner does not as a general rule provide any capital equipment, there is no reason to fear that the abolition of large or absentee land ownership will result in a decline of productivity.[16]

Insofar as it promotes more intensive cultivation, small-unit

---

[13] United Nations, Department of Economic Affairs, *Land Reform: Defects in Agrarian Structure as Obstacles to Economic Development* (New York, 1951), pp. 69–73; Klein, *op. cit.*, pp. 13, 192.

[14] Klein, *op. cit.*, p. 191.

[15] *Ibid.*, p. 13.

[16] United Nations, *Land Reform*, p. 69. Some European peasants, however, lost a great deal in the way of real income as a result of land reform. In Germany, Russia, and Hungary many of the large landowners were excellent and efficient farm managers and were primarily responsible for agricultural innovation and for supplying capital. When the large estates were broken up after World War I, agricultural output fell sharply (see Frederich O. Hertz, *The Economic Problem of the Danubian States: A Study in Economic Nationalism* [London: Victor Gollancz, 1947], pp. 114–118).

farming tends to increase the volume of employment and the total output per acre, as well as savings. Doreen Warriner, emphasizing the merits of peasant farming, has this to say:

The peasant farmer, on the other hand, must regard his family labour as a fixed factor—something which must be maintained whether working or not—and he will try therefore to fill in spare time by keeping live-stock which will add to his output and will utilize this fixed factor more fully. His earnings per hour may be less than on the big farm, but his total earnings will certainly be bigger. Consequently, peasant farming means a better utilization of the labour force. . . . By intensifying live-stock production, the family farm also tends to maintain the fertility of the soil. These important aspects, the un-utilized labor supply and the maintenance of soil fertility, are too often neglected in a discussion of the relative efficiency of capitalistic and family farms.[17]

Bhatnagar, in his study of the Indian rural economy, also emphasizes that small holdings support a larger number of persons and that small holders tend to save more.[18]

Land reform in Korea has created many more small holdings; the number of "half-land tenants" (i.e., those peasants tilling land of which half or less was their own property) was reduced by 77 per cent, while the number of "half-to-full owners" increased by 171 per cent. Ownership of about 26 per cent of the cultivated land in Korea was transferred from absentee landlords to the tillers of the land.[19] These numerous new small holdings have not changed techniques of production or the physical layout of land-holdings. To this extent the land reforms have had no effect on the basic agricultural structure.

Some economists believe that neither have the land reforms increased the volume of employment, as farming was already so intensified that there was little possibility of further increasing employment without increasing capital.[20] But this belief does not seem to be completely justified. The creation of a large number of small, family-owned farms must have inevitably exerted some

[17] Doreen Warriner, *Economics of Peasant Farming* (London: Oxford University Press, 1939), p. 148.
[18] Bhatnagar, *op. cit.*, p. 113.
[19] Klein, *op. cit.*, pp. 108, 192.
[20] Lee, *op. cit.*, p. 55; United Nations, *Land Reform*, p. 91. See also Warriner, *op. cit.*, p. 163.

TABLE 14

NET FARM OUTPUT PER ACRE AND NET NONFARM OUTPUT PER FAMILY MEMBER, KOREA,[a] 1959

(In *hwan*)

Average farm size (in acres)	Farm product			Total farm cost	Net farm output per acre	Net crop output per acre	Average family size	Total farm product	Per capita output	Total nonfarm product	Total nonfarm cost	Net nonfarm output	Net nonfarm output per family member
	Crop	Noncrop	Total										
1.016	206,514	35,506	242,020	73,553	165,814	203,261	5.32	242,020	45,492	44,814	5,820	38,994	7,330
1.847	328,028	48,989	377,018	177,318	140,607	177,600	6.39	377,018	59,001	58,180	19,508	38,672	6,052
3.102	510,563	64,674	575,239	188,458	124,688	164,572	7.43	575,239	77,421	59,537	13,155	46,382	6,243
4.212	615,964	65,611	681,576	222,064	109,095	146,240	8.40	681,576	81,140	61,206	18,489	42,717	5,085
6.056	916,398	97,260	1,013,658	348,303	103,868	151,212	8.63	1,013,658	117,457	110,485	31,067	79,418	9,203
Average													
2.122	361,662	49,984	411,645	131,353	132,088	170,434	6.40	411,645	64,320	56,554	13,847	42,707	6,673

[a] 60 farm districts.

NOTE. Because of rounding, individual figures do not necessarily add up to total.

SOURCE: Bank of Korea, Research Department, *Economic Statistic Year Book*, 1960, pp. 286-289.

effect on the volume of employment and the output per acre. This
effect is illustrated in table 14, which shows that the smaller the
farm, the larger the output per acre because of the more intensive
use of labor. As total output is increased by the redistribution of
land into small holdings, it may be justifiable, from an economic
standpoint, at least, to defend the small farm. This argument,
however, can be advanced only if there are no alternative employment opportunities and no offsetting drawbacks to small-farm
operation.

The higher per capita output on the larger farms reflects a
greater availability of capital, and the higher per acre output on
the smaller farms results from more intensive cultivation by means
of labor used more intensively. The scale of operation of the small
farm is so limited that adherence to it will perpetuate the static
condition of the rural economy. The smallness of the farm itself
does not offer incentives for improving the method and the organization of production. The present relatively large output per
acre is mainly the result of hard manual labor with very rudi-
mentary methods and organization. The smallness of the farm is
often responsible for waterlogging, soil erosion, and the increased
scattering of the holding.

THE OPTIMUM SIZE OF FARM HOLDINGS

The optimum size of a farm must lie somewhere between the
smallest and the largest holding. This size cannot, however, be
decided purely on technical grounds, for it is inevitable that the
prevailing social organization must be taken into account. There
are more self-supporting family laborers on the larger farm. When
plenty of labor is available as a substitute for machines and tools,
saving for capital investment tends to be neglected. In Korean
agriculture, as the size of the farm increases, the output per acre
becomes smaller and the tendency to save also becomes less (see
appendix table 4). We conclude, therefore, that under existing
social institutions farms larger than three acres and smaller than
two acres are not optimal. If the optimum size of holding obtained throughout the rural area, total output would be increased
without changing the factor supply and with no further changes in

the method and the organization of production. Although this is one vital step toward development of the economy without altering the conditions of factor supply and without introducing new technology, the attainment of this optimum size of holdings would require governmental intervention and would not leave the society *in statu quo.*

DIVERSIFICATION, COÖPERATIVES, AND SMALL HANDICRAFT INDUSTRIES

In the rest of this chapter we shall consider (1) diversification of agricultural products, (2) credit coöperatives, and (3) small handicraft industries as possible methods of improving the employment situation within the agricultural community.

1) Diversification of production may appear to be one way of obtaining a higher scale of living. Agricultural activity could be expanded into livestock, poultry, dairy products, industrial crops, and fruits and vegetables. The limited demand in urban areas for the diversified products, however, inhibits such a development. It has been a conventional view that urban industries do not expand because nearly two-thirds of the people live in rural areas and lack sufficient purchasing power for industrial products. It is a vicious circle, for agriculture fails to progress and its demand for industrial products fails to grow because of the lack of urban demand for more diversified rural products. The cattle and the horses presently available are used mostly for farm work. In addition, Buddhism does not permit a meat diet to monks. The demand for meat products is correspondingly limited. Even poultry and smaller animals, such as pigs, sheep, and goats, are relatively unimportant in comparison with cereal crops (see appendix table 3).[21] The climate is not favorable for fodder grass, and the existing wild grass is of low quality.

A further obstacle to diversification is the high cost of raising animals. An animal consumes from five to eight pounds of cereals in order to produce a pound of meat; yet a pound of meat goes no

---

[21] The major protein food of most Koreans is fish, which collect in the water of the rice paddies, in ponds and rivers, and in the seas surrounding the Korean peninsula.

further in maintaining a man's life than a pound of cereals.[22] The return from such investment is negative in terms of life-sustaining food. Unless there is a market for meat outside the agricultural community, one cannot expect farmers to expand by sacrificing some of their crop production. "As the Preparatory Commission on World Food Proposals of the United Nations Food and Agriculture Organization pointed out in its report published in 1947: 'The buying power of the non-agricultural population must rise at a speed which matches the increase in food production so that food can be paid for at reasonable prices.' " [23]

TABLE 15

THE NUTRITIVE VALUE OF VARIOUS CROPS, IN TERMS OF CALORIES

Crop	Number of calories produced per *tan* (.245 acres)	Number of days calorie production per *tan* can feed adult requiring 2,400 calories per day
Rice	896,948	374
Barley	682,020	284
Wheat	578,054	241
Beans	346,628	144
Potatoes	875,760	365
Sweet potatoes	1,461,600	609

SOURCE: Shiroshi Nasu, *Land Utilization in Japan* (Chicago: University of Chicago Press, 1929), p. 192.

Diversification of some products is further limited because of tastes. In Korea, tobacco, vegetables (especially sweet potatoes), and fruit give comparatively higher yields than dry-field grain. But these high-yield crops have a limited domestic market.[24] Table 15 shows that the sweet potatoes are especially rich in health-supporting nutritive elements. If taste could be changed, the economy would gain substantially, in terms of calorie production, from the cultivation of this vegetable.

[22] Howard, *op. cit.*, p. 19.
[23] International Labour Office, *The Economic Background of Social Policy including Problems of Industrialisation*, Report IV (New Delhi, 1947), p. 164; and for similar reasoning also cf. United Nations, *Land Reform*, p. 73.
[24] Korea, Ministry of Reconstruction, *Economic Survey*, 1959 (Seoul, 1959), p. 77.

2) Agricultural coöperatives are often suggested as a way of improving a stagnant rural community. The pooling of savings could be a means of securing needed things which individual farmers cannot afford; or the pooling of effort could improve a farm group's trading position vis-à-vis the rest of the economy. The coöperative, however, has never prospered in Korea, even though the government has encouraged and assisted the farmers in this direction. One reason for the lack of success of coöperatives has been the smallness of the scale of individual farm operation. As each individual farmer has plenty of labor and little to sell, he has limited incentives to join a coöperative.

3) Light handicraft industries in rural Korea also encounter serious obstacles. These industries are characterized by antiquated methods and small-scale, hand operation. Power-driven machines are rarely used. Generally, labor working with a small set of simple primitive tools is the only source of power. Again the smallness of scale of such operations provides little scope for division of labor. Consequently very low productivity and unstandardized output are the rule.[25] Small-scale handicraft industries have been disappearing steadily as a result of competition from modern factory industry at home and abroad.

Traditional handicraft industries in the Korean farm household produce straw rope, mats, and bamboo and wooden products. The nature of these industries accounts for the fact that they exist only in areas that are not in competition with modern urban factory industries. Hand spinning in rural Korea has virtually disappeared. Only the very poorest families engage in spinning, and only for their own use, not for marketing purposes.

The hand-loom industries (e.g., cotton and silk spinning) in China and India, as well as in Korea, were the first to be affected by the competition from modern mills. Raising silkworms and cocoons is an entirely rural occupation, but even this sphere of activity has steadily declined because of the long-term competition of Japan and because of the appearance of synthetic fibers. In Morocco, Tunisia, and Algeria, also, the formerly prosperous

---

[25] Of course, this does not apply to advanced countries like Switzerland (watchmaking), Czechoslovakia (glass and jewelry industries), and, to a lesser degree, Japan (silk and potash, handicrafts, etc.).

handicraft industries, such as the tarboosh industry, seem about to become extinct.[26]

In modern times each item produced by hand is expected to meet a certain standard. Quality control is crucial. Careful designing, precision, and a high standard of uniformity in the manufactured components are required to compete with modern factory methods. The market for nonstandardized goods has been declining. Even the small village workshop in Switzerland has had some difficulty.[27] The problem of standardization, according to Meier, imposes a geographical limitation on the expansion of these industries: "Only those towns and hamlets lying along the main roads, or close to the center of commerce, may be expected to participate in this pattern of industrialization."[28] In summary, light and mobile industries as potential users of part-time employment in the village are not numerous because of excessive factory competition.

The continuation of small-scale handicraft industries seems to depend, in large measure, on assistance provided by the government, such as direct subsidies, reduction of land income taxes, improvement in rural credit institutions, training of skilled and managerial personnel, coördinating methods for standardization, and protection from home and foreign competition. The International Labour Office has taken the same view: "The establishment of local small-scale industries on a nationwide basis will probably prove a much more difficult task than the development of large-scale industries . . . and demand more in the way of government assistance and organization."[29] The present outlook for these industries in Korea is very bleak. According to the sample inquiry, the gross income per farm household from handicrafts, in 1959, amounted to about 1.2 per cent of its gross farm proceeds, and about 10 per cent of the gross noncrop income.

Rather than further encourage these handicraft industries, in an effort to absorb idle labor in off seasons and to provide for addi-

[26] "The Promotion of Handicrafts in North Africa," *International Labour Review*, LXXVII (Jan., 1958), 60.

[27] Richard L. Meier, *Science and Economic Development: New Patterns of Living* (New York: John Wiley & Sons, 1956), p. 171.

[28] *Ibid.*

[29] "The Promotion of Handicrafts in North Africa," p. 176.

tional income at government expense, modern factory industry should be speeded up. These traditional light industries have undergone a natural extinction through competitive forces from outside. If they cannot be carried out efficiently enough to meet the competition at home and abroad, it is unwise to encourage them. This point is extremely important in view of the fact that any capital employed in the traditional handicraft industries would remain idle in peak agricultural seasons. Labor scarcity in such seasons would surely create this incongruous condition of capital waste. It is, therefore, unwise to frame a policy that would keep expensive capital, instead of cheap labor, employed for only part of the year. In other words, a labor-intensive rather than capital-intensive method should be the choice in programing economic development of the agricultural sector. John Lossing Buck says that China invests labor, the United States, capital; if the cost of capital were compared with the cheapness of labor, some "waste" of labor would not be so serious an economic loss.[30]

The decline of handicraft industries is uncritically and consistently mourned by sociologists on the ground that it has resulted in a loss of employment opportunities and "necessitated profound changes in social institutions and in the scale of values" by which the rural people have lived for centuries.[31] I contend, however, that such grief is unjustified. As long as output is produced within the country, or imported in exchange for exports, the economy as a whole will be better off; the induced changes in social institutions and in their value system may bring about profoundly beneficial effects. Output could be increased by breaking up traditional social institutions, which are obstacles to enhanced economic motivations and the mobility of labor, as well as to the propensity to save. Provided the decline of rural industries results from the growth of modern industries or from greater international specialization, the loss of rural employment by the decline of handicraft and light industries can be more than compensated for by the gains from the new development.

---

[30] John Lossing Buck, *Chinese Farm Economy* (Chicago: University of Chicago Press, 1930), p. 313.

[31] "The Promotion of Handicrafts in North Africa," p. 174.

CONCLUSION

Farming in rice-growing regions has frequently been described as "static" or "fixed." [32] In this chapter I have elaborated on some of the conditions that account for this static or fixed nature of Korean agriculture, with its background of the family-clan-village system, and ecological conditions. These factors stand in the way of change. Yet change is an absolute necessity for the improvement of labor conditions and of the scale of living. As it is impossible to institute an effective change under the present social, economic, and technical conditions, a workable development program will require, first, a fundamental change in these conditions, which in turn would require extra capital. It is, however, outside the scope of this study to recommend a development program that would call for extra capital. What must be found, then, is a way to improve the rural economy which would not entail extra capital. The attempt to solve this problem will be made in chapter vii.

---

[32] See, for example, Warriner, *op. cit.*, p. 97.

VII

Surplus Labor and
Real Capital Formation

In chapters iv and v, two kinds of underemployment in Korean agriculture were investigated. It was found that tradition-directed underemployment was, *ceteris paribus,* not available for permanent withdrawal from the land, but that technical underemployment was truly surplus labor and was withdrawable from the land. Technical underemployment was primarily due to lack of sufficient work, a lack primarily attributable to deep-rooted technical inadequacies, whereas tradition-directed underemployment was due to the influence of deep-rooted institutions. In this chapter I shall further analyze the policy implications of these two kinds of idle labor, in connection with the possibility of drawing some of both kinds away from the land.

Korean agriculture exhibits a severe scarcity of capital and other technical means of production, in sharp contrast to an abundance of labor available for farming in off seasons. The problem is how to utilize this idle labor more fully so that economic development may be pushed to a higher level. The crux of the problem is to investigate the possibility of the use of a wider range of factor proportions.[1] The necessity of finding alternative production processes becomes more urgent because of the peculiar char-

[1] R. S. Eckaus, "The Factor Proportions Problem in Underdeveloped Areas," *American Economic Review,* XLV (Sept., 1955), 561–565.

acteristics of the rural labor structure. The family-clan-village system, religion, conservatism, lack of experimentation, inertia, poverty, undernourishment, and lack of education all contribute to the lack of labor mobility. The absence of greater labor mobility limits the range of possible factor combinations and restricts a fuller utilization of available resources. In order to make labor more mobile, changes in the value system are necessary. This could be done by increasing the demand for rural labor by urban industries, by mass education, or through other governmental measures, that is, by relaxing the *ceteris paribus* assumption about given technical means of production.

The problem of factor proportions becomes still more difficult because at times there is too much work to be done, and at other times, too little. While labor is fully employed in agricultural work, nonagricultural capital will necessarily be idle. Development programing must take this fact into consideration. The problem of employment or underemployment in such an economy is not only seasonal and technical (open) but also tradition-directed (closed). To draw the tradition-directed underemployed off the land requires social and/or economic changes. This is the reason for advocating that, in the early stage of economic development, available capital must be utilized for providing jobs for those regarded as the technical (open) underemployed.

THE NURKSE PLAN

Nurkse's proposal for withdrawing labor from the land really amounts to advocacy of compulsory labor. His plan may be carried out either by directly mobilizing labor or by levying a tax on so-called "disguised saving" (the consumption of those who constitute disguised unemployment), which can be used to finance projects for utilizing idle labor. Under a compulsory scheme like this, there is no problem of open or closed underemployment. All one has to know is who is idle. But the probable pattern might well be to put the hand on the poor instead of the rich. This kind of discrimination would occur because more of the poor are openly idle simply because they do not have capital to work with. Such a scheme cannot be justified on humanitarian grounds, nor is it politically advisable. N. Koestner comments on Nurkse's proposal as follows:

Practically every ray of hope the lecturer [Nurkse] shows us is combined with application to the toiling masses of coercion, restrictions on consumption, increased taxation, etc. . . . Whether it is the redirection of labour force from villages to dig canals, or industrialization à la Japan or Soviet Russia, or the forced saving on starvation levels by means of inflation or stricter taxation, it is always the toiling man who has to suffer additional (if sometimes only relative) burdens.[2]

Professor Nurkse was especially ill-advised to have delivered his lecture in Egypt, where there are many historical examples of forced labor being imposed on the abjectly poor. Nurkse's proposals are of course aimed at helping indigent people, but one cannot help wondering if the "cure" might not be worse than the "disease."

The solution of levying a tax on "disguised savings" is equally questionable, but for other reasons. Such a tax levy would not be so simple in practice as Nurkse suggests. In the first place, the tax should not be levied *before* the labor is withdrawn. As consumption must not be reduced further in the interval between taxation and the actual employment of labor in a capital project, a reserve fund is necessary to operate this scheme. Moreover, Nurkse's type of capital formation actually requires a substantial amount of extra capital for administrative and technical costs. The possibility of employing idle labor without making expenditures for certain kinds of training for new jobs, for additional tools to work with, for housing, and for other industrial overhead capital is limited.[3] In rural Korea farmers are often mobilized to construct and maintain the highways and community irrigation projects near the workers' residences (see appendix table 1). This compulsory work is of course carried out without compensation, and closeness to the village is a necessary condition for its imposition. Finally, as noted in chapter iv, if projects involve heavier types of work, food requirements in terms of caloric intake must be substantially increased. According to Koestner, citing the Egyptian situation, the

---

[2] N. Koestner, "Some Comments on Professor Nurkse's Capital Accumulation in Underdeveloped Countries," *L'Egypte Contemporaine*, XLIV (April, 1953), 18.

[3] Gerald M. Meier and Robert E. Baldwin, *Economic Development: Theory History, Policy* (New York: John Wiley & Sons, 1957), p. 342.

government must find at least 1,200 extra calories a day per worker, or 41 per cent more than idle laborers could possibly bring along with them when they are employed on these projects, in order to raise idle labor to the level of full employment on an eight-hour daily basis.[4]

This can be understood by illustrating Koestner's method of calculating the extra food requirement. Let us assume that one-third of the farm workers are idle, and, further, that this third need only a survival level of 1,700 calories a day, and that the remaining two-thirds need a full daily ration of, say, 2,900 calories. The average consumption, before launching a capital project, is $1/3 \times 1,700 + 2/3 \times 2,900 = 2,500$ calories, which is already substantially more than the average daily consumption per person in the entire population (2,200 calories). If the idle one-third of the workers are mobilized for, say, irrigation or flood control projects near the village, they must also now consume 2,900 calories a day, or about 16 per cent more than their share of food before the capital project (2,500 calories). All workers—those remaining on the farm, who now have to work harder and longer, and those on the capital project—must now consume 2,900 calories. Nurkse's disguised saving will then be 1,700 calories per worker, not 2,500 calories. The government must therefore find an extra 1,200 calories, or 41 per cent more per worker employed on the capital project. Koestner adds to this figure an extra 25 per cent of the calorie cost per workman for administrative and other costs. This brings the total to 3,625 calories; consequently the government must find an extra 1,925 calories.[5] If this is multiplied by the number of workers withdrawn from the land, we arrive at the total extra food requirement.

Koestner's estimate on this aggregate basis does perhaps exaggerate the extra food requirement. The per capita food supply in Egypt (2,570 calories) is much more favorable than in Korea (2,200 calories). As the worker must consume somewhat more than the nonworker (children, old people, etc.), the average consumption of the Egyptian worker must be somewhat more than 2,500 calories.[6] In this circumstance, if the ration for the fully employed

[4] Koestner, *op. cit.*, pp. 9–10.

[5] *Ibid.*

[6] This assumes no great differences between Egypt and Korea in the ratio of workers to inactive population.

is still 2,900 calories, the lowest level of consumption is probably above 1,700 calories. Then the difference between this bottom consumption and the full-employment consumption must be narrower. Koestner's estimate seems more valid for Korea than for Egypt, provided it applies only to the worker in rural Korea, for the average per capita consumption of Korean urban workers is approximately 2,500 calories. Egyptian workers' per capita consumption must be more than 2,500 calories.[7]

Nurkse's original scheme does not distinguish between permanent withdrawal and intermittent withdrawal of labor after seasonal employment. This distinction is extremely important if a program is to be truly feasible. It is impossible to withdraw any labor permanently if, as in Korea, there could be an actual seasonal shortage of labor. If the labor shortage were eliminated by reducing the peak labor requirement, there would be some chronic underemployment that could be permanently withdrawn. How could this be achieved?

A WAY OF OBTAINING A CHRONIC EXCESS OF LABOR

The possibility of reducing the peak labor requirement is usually discussed in terms of additional capital investment, substantial change in the product mix, or a different method and organization of production. These changes, however, are not practicable under present social, economic, and technical conditions. The necessary conditions that make mechanization a successful substitute for labor are absent. Some of the major obstacles that stand in the way of mechanization are the relative abundance of labor; small, scattered, fragmented, and, in many instances, terraced fields; and the nature of rice cultivation. Moreover, even if mechanization were suitable for small, scattered, and fragmented holdings, the composition of labor would have to be changed in

---

[7] Note also that an increase in consumption by workers remaining on the farm is unavoidable. The remaining farmers must consume more than before, because they have to do more work. This point has been raised by Koestner and Leibenstein. Koestner, however, does not recognize Leibenstein's point that an increase in consumption may lead to a total output more than proportionate to the increased consumption.

order to reap the full benefit of mechanization. The labor on which the farmer depends is not usually hired labor but mostly family labor, and hence there would be no visible saving from mechanization.[8] Thus mechanization may be delayed for as long as these social institutions are an accepted way of life.

Neither can coöperative farming among the people of the village eliminate the labor shortage. The "labor coöperative," on a voluntary basis, is already an accepted practice. In fact, the employment of some wage labor in addition to the labor exchange, and the mobilization of inactive members of the family, are necessary to meet the deficit of family labor in peak seasons. Thus we begin to understand Bhatnagar's conclusion that "the amount of labor that must be retained in agriculture would be much greater than was expected." [9]

Many farming practices are antiquated and inefficient. As agricultural skill in such countries is handed down, unchanged, for generations, human physical performance may be very underproductive.[10] Louise Howard attributes such inefficiency to the absence of good, systematic instruction, that is, to the lack of intelligent preparation for manual work. Inefficient ways of doing things can be improved by training and education, but this would require extra capital.

That so many obstacles stand in the way of reducing the peak labor requirement, however, does not eliminate entirely the possibility of obtaining a chronic state of idle labor. The calculation, in chapter v, of the amount of idle labor was based on an acceptance of the time distribution of food consumption in quantity and quality: as in peak agricultural seasons food consumption is usually lower than in off seasons, we assumed that farm workers are physically not capable of working more than eight hours a day in the busy season. It is possible, however, to reduce the labor shortage by providing more and better food in these peak months. Suppose that farm laborers work ten hours a day instead of eight in peak seasons, because they eat better food which results in better health. Then there would be chronic idle

---

[8] Kalka P. Bhatnagar *et al.*, *Indian Rural Economy* (Parade-Kanpur: Kishore Publishing House, 1955), p. 139.

[9] *Ibid.*, p. 147.

[10] Louise E. Howard, *Labour in Agriculture: An International Survey* (London: Oxford University Press, 1935), p. 230.

labor of farm workers amounting to about 17 per cent of the labor available in June, or about 175 persons, in terms of equivalent man-hours, within the sample population.[11] It must be noted that the figure 175 applies not only to the month of June but also to the other months. As there is more idle labor in the other eleven months than in June, the peak month, there is no problem of needing any of these 175 persons in any other month.

This notion can be clearly understood by using Hsieh Chiang's formula for computing "visible underemployment." [12] By applying our concept of underemployment, we find that 67 persons are technically (openly) unemployed, and the rest (108 persons) are tradition-directed (closed) underemployed. Provided the sample is reasonably representative, the amount of idle labor in the entire agricultural community is approximately 690,000 farm workers.[13] This is a substantial number of laborers who could be dispensed with in farming. Assuming that one farm worker is accompanied by his family of 3.468 additional persons,[14] the total number of people involved—workers and their families—is approximately 2.39 million, which is about 20 per cent of the entire farming population.[15]

A readjustment of food distribution is desirable. The extra food supply in June, July, and October will lead to an increased saving of labor, for some of the labor in off seasons is available for alternative uses in any event. The present grain control by the Korean government (shown in appendix table 5) is not concerned with this problem. Although about 32 per cent of the grain collected from the farmers was given back to them, the primary aim of the return was not seasonal adjustment of food consumption.

---

[11] In the sample, the total idle labor on a ten-hour basis amounted to 43,636 hours in June; the labor available per farm worker in the same month was 250 hours. The figure 175 is arrived at by dividing the former by the latter.

[12] Chiang's formula for showing the relationship between seasonal and chronic underemployment is $U = \dfrac{A - 12P}{A} - \dfrac{11(P - O)}{A}$ where U indicates the extent of visible underemployment; A, the amount of labor available; P, the amount of employed labor in the month of peak activity; and O, the average amount of labor employed per month in off seasons (Hsieh Chiang, "Underemployment in Asia. I. Nature and Extent," *International Labour Review*, LXV [June, 1952], 708).

[13] This is based on 569 sample farm households in June, from a total of 2,245,161.

[14] The number of farm workers per household in June was 1.86 persons, and the average number of persons per family was 6.45.

[15] The total full-time farming population was about 12 million in 1959. The population of Korea in the same year was about 22.9 million.

It is, however, conceded that voluntary instead of governmental measures seem more plausible. As the amount of food left over after selling some to finance other essential living expenses is very limited, the reduction of food consumption in off seasons may be impossible. Moreover, the administrative cost to the government of handling the taxed grain would be very high.

In passing, it is noted that people in underdeveloped agricultural countries are at the present time more deprived than is usually realized. Economists often talk about "human investment" in terms of education. But in underdeveloped countries today human investment in terms of health seems more urgent. A substantial share of any available fund for human investment must go first into the maintenance of better health.

A DETERRENT TO PERMANENT WITHDRAWAL OF LABOR FROM THE LAND

There is a major difficulty in the permanent withdrawal of labor from the land: the substantial difference in living costs between rural and urban areas. Table 16 shows the difference between living expenditures per family member for the farm family and for the wage laborer's family in Seoul.[16] The rural farm household spent, on the average, about 62,000 *hwan* per family member in 1959; in the same year the urban household spent more than twice as much, or about 135,000 *hwan*. This is an important reason that farmers have been so reluctant to leave rural areas for urban employment.

Because a reasonable comparison of this kind must, however, be carried out on the assumption of identical labor in terms of quality, and must also take into consideration the price differentials for commodities and services, it may be assumed that only the families of urban wage laborers who earn less than 480,000 *hwan,* or families that spend about 92,000 *hwan* per member of the family on living expenditures, are roughly comparable with the average rural farm household. Urban wage laborers who maintain an average per capita expenditure of 92,000 *hwan* are pre-

---

[16] Urban areas other than Seoul may be more pertinent to the comparison, but no other comparable data are available at present.

TABLE 16
Comparison of Living Expenditures in Rural and Urban Households per Member of Family, Korea, 1959
(In *hwan*)

	Rural						Urban[a]			
	Average						Average	4.7 less than 480,000	5.7 480,000 to 719,999	6.4 720,000 to 959,999
Size of farm (in acres)	2.122	1.016	1.847	3.102	4.212	6.056				
Size of family	6.4	5.32	6.39	7.43	8.40	8.63	6.1	4.7	5.7	6.4
Net total income before tax	417,988	284,253	426,936	518,412	642,437	880,137	—	480,000	719,999	959,999
Living expenditure per member of family	61,942	52,779	59,793	63,832	69,914	95,689	135,160	91,972	127,641	136,885
Food	33,889	31,376	32,376	33,852	37,263	48,651	58,414	47,711	56,941	64,785
Housing	1,739	1,183	1,868	1,927	2,231	2,410	21,701	13,699	18,283	24,340
Fuel and light	8,727	8,081	8,253	9,099	9,581	11,187	8,684	8,068	8,123	8,457
Clothing	5,073	4,270	4,907	5,291	5,859	7,642	12,130	5,356	8,969	11,745
Luxuries[b]	2,475	1,625	2,426	2,575	2,819	4,951	8,074	4,001	5,771	5,568
Education	2,628	1,332	2,674	2,536	2,899	7,428	2,828	1,528	2,057	2,914
Others[c]	7,411	4,912	7,289	8,552	9,262	13,420	23,329	11,609	27,497	19,076

[a] Only the lowest three income brackets are listed; the average is, however, for all income brackets.
[b] Includes entertainment, celebration, culture, recreation, and so forth.
[c] Includes health, sanitation, communication, trasportation, and incidental expenses.
Source: Bank of Korea, Research Department.

sumably unskilled workers. When ordinary farm workers are transferred to capital projects, they will, by and large, not be able to do any better than wage laborers who earn the least in urban areas.

Although the lowest-earning urban wage laborers spend about one-third more than the rural average, they are not better off in real terms. A careful observation of both kinds of living expenditures provides a clue to understanding this problem. Table 16 shows that housing and food expenditures of the lowest-earning urban wage laborers are substantially higher than those of the average rural family. But because of the gap in prices there is actually no difference in the scale of living. Rural people in Korea tend to spend more on education than on luxury goods and services—an interesting contrast with the spending habits of urban wage laborers. The aggregate expenditure for fuel, light, clothing, education, and luxuries is about the same for both the average farm family and the poorest urban wage laborer's family. And, although the unidentified expenditures ("Others" in table 16) are larger in urban areas, examination shows that a large part of these expenditures—transportation, communication, health, and so on— are extra costs necessary to urban life as compared with rural life. Therefore the average scale of living of rural people is approximately the same as that of wage laborers in the lowest income bracket in Seoul, despite the fact that the latter spend about one-third more than the former.

For this reason, when the permanent withdrawal of labor is undertaken, withdrawn farm workers must be guaranteed at least the same level of earning that the lowest-earning wage laborer's family in urban areas enjoys: an annual living expenditure of about 92,000 *hwan* per member of the family. In other words, the farm worker who gives up his farming for employment in urban capital projects must have about one-third more than he had for his previous living expenditures. In the permanent withdrawal of idle labor, allowance must be made for these higher living expenditures.

The extra capital requirement for the permanent withdrawal of idle labor would be enormous. The extra living expenditures of the workers themselves would amount to about 18,810 million *hwan;* additional living expenses of the workers' families would amount to 73,500 million *hwan.*[17] The aggregate figure would therefore be approximately 92,310 million *hwan,* or about 15.2 per cent of government expenditures—608,723 million *hwan*—for fiscal 1959. Additional expenditures would be needed for building houses for the workers, for training them, and for other fixed administrative costs.

To conclude, the permanent withdrawal of idle labor is not feasible at present, especially in view of the fact that there are also large amounts of unemployment and underemployment in urban areas. The withdrawal of idle labor in off seasons only will preclude the need for labor-saving devices in peak agricultural seasons. In off seasons laborers can be mobilized for projects that can be carried out near their homes. But there still remains the question of how such projects are to be financed. Let us consider the answer to this question in the following chapter.

---

[17] The extra living expenditure of workers is computed by multiplying 30,000 *hwan,* the extra urban living expenditure per person, by 627,000, the number of technical (open) idle laborers. And the extra living expenditure of the worker's family is computed by multiplying 30,000 *hwan* by the number of accompanying members of the workers' families, 2.45 million persons.

VIII

A Proposed Program

A change in the stagnant society of rural Korea is urgently needed. The rationale of the program outlined in this chapter to improve the prevailing socioeconomic conditions is that development policies must aim at the utmost utilization of idle labor within the scope of the limited resources currently available. Moreover, the program is designed to help initiate the gradual dissolution of the underlying social institutions to which I have attributed the very conditions of extensive tradition-directed underemployment, immobility of labor, little or no savings, and low productivity of land. It is also anticipated that the program will bring the size of the average farm nearer to the optimum. The social institutions, the size of families, and the size of farms react upon one another and are interdependent; a beneficial change in the first will react favorably upon the other two.

Projects that do not require additional training of labor and that will be within walking distance of villages must be introduced. The former condition is necessary to obviate the need of capital for training, and the latter, to enable the workers to perform farm labor and project labor without spending too much time in getting from one place of work to the other. Therefore, projects to promote irrigation, to build small dams, and to achieve reforestation would best serve the purpose.

As the number and the size of projects are limited by the availability of funds, efficiency necessitates a careful program evaluation. The Korean government classifies agricultural projects into three categories: technical developments, capital developments, and others. The first includes improvement of seeds, fertilizers, methods of cultivation, and the like; the second includes various measures that improve and reconstruct farm land, such as dams and irrigation projects. The last category, "others," comprises such things as fertilizer distribution, product inspection, and statistical research. This discussion will be confined to capital improvement projects.

JUSTIFICATION FOR GIVING PREFERENCE TO CAPITAL IMPROVEMENT PROJECTS

This study has led to a strong inference that priority should be given to capital investment in the agricultural sector rather than elsewhere in the economy. Recent experience shows that the return from this type of capital investment can be very high within a short period.[1] Table 17 presents specific information about the capital-output ratios of farm-land development projects: the capital-output ratio was 0.7 in 1955, 1.9 in 1956, 1.6 in 1957, and 2.1 in 1958. The average ratio for the four years was 1.8.[2]

Of course, the capital-output ratio on a gross output basis (i.e., without deducting operating costs) is a crude one. But in view of the fact that there is much idle labor and that the plan is to use the idle labor near the villages, it may safely be assumed that the social cost of employing idle labor is near zero.[3] Therefore a good case can be made on the basis of the capital-output ratio. Some incremental capital-output ratio is always implicit in any development plan. A capital-output ratio of 1.7 for rice farm-land

---

[1] For a useful analysis of investment choice by the marginal-internal-rate-of-return method, see Roland N. McKean, *Efficiency in Government through Systems Analysis: With Emphasis on Water Resources Development* (New York: John Wiley & Sons, 1958), chaps. 1, 5.

[2] Unfortunately, as the data on farming costs are not available at present, the net rate of return from investment cannot be calculated. As we are concerned at this moment only with the farming cost of rice cultivation, the data for farming costs as a whole are not useful. This is why the capital-output ratio is used instead of the internal rate of return. The use of the latter results in the added difficulty of finding a proper discount rate.

[3] For a valuable discussion of this point see Hollis B. Chenery, "The Application of Investment Criteria," *Quarterly Journal of Economics*, LXVII (Feb., 1953), 76–91.

TABLE 17

CAPITAL-OUTPUT RATIO OF FARM-LAND DEVELOPMENT PROJECTS,[a]
KOREA, 1955–1958

Year	Number of project regions	Benefited area (in acres)	Incremental output (in *suk*[b])	Value of incremental output (in millions of *hwan*)	Capital invested (in millions of *hwan*)	Incremental capital-output ratio	Two-year incremental capital-output ratio
1955	86	78,624	79,624	1,484	983	0.7	—
1956	1,139	994,737	183,190	6,109	11,560	1.9	1.7
1957	1,574	393,946	322,065	10,918	17,773	1.6	1.7
1958	1,505	341,932	346,751	9,654	20,685	2.1	1.9
Four-year total				28,165	51,001	1.8	
Cumulative total[c]				55,753	94,844	1.7	

[a] These farm-land development projects are limited to rice paddy fields.

[b] 1 *suk* = 4.96 bushels.

[c] We assume that the same amount of incremental output in each beginning year continues through 1958. Specifically, the 1955 figures are multiplied by 4; the 1956 figures, by 3; the 1957 figures, by 2; and the 1958 figures, by 1.

SOURCE: Bank of Korea, Research Department, *Annual Economic Review*, 1959, sec. 1, p. 45. The totals and the incremental capital-output ratios were estimated by the author.

development projects seems a reasonable estimate, and one that is likely to continue as long as there is unimproved land. Leaving out of account many conceptual and empirical problems in the estimation of such a ratio,[4] there are a few other problems that are particularly relevant to an agricultural country: (1) price changes in estimating the incremental output due to capital projects, and (2) the output lag from the initial investment.[5] The ratio for 1955 is very much underestimated because of the output lag; the ratios for 1956 and 1957 are also somewhat underestimated because of the above two considerations; and finally, the 1958 ratio is underestimated mainly because of the drastic fall in

---

[4] Cf. Benjamin Higgins, *Economic Development: Principles, Problems, and Policies* (New York: W. W. Norton & Co., 1959), pp. 642–648.

[5] In 1956 rice production fell sharply (by about 17 per cent from the 1955 figure) because of weather conditions. This low rice output necessitated an increase of about 150 per cent in the import of foodstuffs. Yet the wholesale price index rose by about 59 per cent. In 1958 rice production increased by 5.4 per cent over the preceding year's record high (since 1945), or by 13.3 per cent over the average rice production of 1953–1957; as a consequence, the price of rice was 18.4 per cent lower than in 1957. As for the output lag, the incremental output in 1955 must have been partially owing to capital projects in the preceding year or years; consequently, the incremental output in each successive year must be considered as partly owing to the preceding year's capital investment.

the price of rice. In order to avoid these difficulties, I have devised two new ways of computing this ratio. One is a cumulative one, another is the two-year average gross incremental capital-output ratio. The latter ranges from 1.7 to 1.9; the former is 1.7.

Let us use a capital-output ratio of 1.7 for calculating capital requirements. For the kind of project under consideration here, even this imprecise ratio is quite useful in decision making. Although the return from the marginal investment has a tendency to decline, either kind of ratio shows that the incremental output from a given capital investment is rather high, despite the fact that Korean rice production is already carried out, uniformly, in an intensive manner. Compared with other economic activities, this agricultural capital-output ratio is low. I estimate that the incremental capital-output ratio for all Korea would range from 2.5 to 3.0.[6] This justifies the contention that first priority should be given to the agricultural sector.

The capital improvements already undertaken in the Korean agricultural sector have also had a very significant effect on the rest of the economy. The increase in rice production in 1958 over 1957, owing to capital improvements, was 1,719,000 bushels, or about 41 per cent of the total incremental output. This increment was a major factor in lowering the price of rice by 18.7 per cent from the preceding year, and also in lowering the general price level of all commodities by 6.2 per cent. Thus, as the Bank

---

[6]

GROSS INCREMENTAL CAPITAL-OUTPUT RATIOS
IN SELECTED COUNTRIES AND INDUSTRIES

Country and Industry	Years	Ratio
Ceylon	1947–1953	2.8
Burma	1947/48–1952/53	5.1
Argentina	1945–1953	5.3
Italy	1947–1954	2.9
India	1948/49–1953/54	3.2
Cement		3.0–3.5
Pulp and paper		3.5–4.0
Iron and steel		3.5–4.0
Agriculture		1.0
United States	1947–1954	5.0
Trade and service		0.1 or less
Manufacture		1.3–2.0
Housing and public utilities		10 or more

SOURCE: Benjamin Higgins, *Economic Development: Principles, Problems, and Policies* (New York: W. W. Norton & Co., 1959), pp. 22, 646.

of Korea views it, such capital improvements undertaken in the rural community are cornerstones of anti-inflation and economic stability.[7]

There is still much improvement to be made in rural Korea. In 1958, as table 18 shows, only about 52 per cent of the land was completely irrigated; a little more than half of the remainder

TABLE 18

IRRIGATION AND PRODUCTIVITY, KOREA, 1958

Degree of irrigation	Land area[a]	Rice production[a]	Output of rice per unit of land[b]
Completely irrigated	51.9	58.5	142.7
Partly irrigated	24.8	23.3	119.1
Nonirrigated	23.3	18.2	100.0

[a] In percentages of total.
[b] The output of rice per unit of nonirrigated land = 100.
SOURCE: Korea, Bank of Korea, Research Department, *Annual Economic Review*, 1959, sec. 1, pp. 47–48.

was partly irrigated, and the rest was left entirely to the mercy of the elements. Potential capital improvement projects are not confined, of course, to irrigation per se. The building of embankments, the reclamation of land, and the like are also capital improvements.

THE FARM HOUSEHOLD BUDGET

Study of the economic profile of farm households is a prelude to making specific proposals for financing capital improvements (see farm family budget for 1959, table 19). Without donations and subsidies, farmers, no matter what the size of their holdings, could not maintain even the low existing scale of living. They would have deficits in their family budgets (see the last line of table 19) ranging from 3.3 to 14.4 per cent of per capita living expenditures. Understandably, the smaller the farm, the more urgent the need

---

[7] Bank of Korea, Research Department, *Annual Economic Review*, 1959 (Seoul, 1959), sec. 1, p. 47.

TABLE 19

FARM FAMILY BUDGET, KOREA,[a] 1959

(In *hwan*)

Size of sample	227	194	81	46	34	582 (total)
Size of family	5.32	6.39	7.43	8.40	8.63	6.40 (average)
Average size of farm (in acres)	1.016	1.847	3.102	4.212	6.056	2.122 (average)
Total net income per household[b]	284,253	426,936	518,412	642,437	880,137	417,988 (average)
Earned income	258,061	395,321	507,295	619,855	855,684	392,419 (average)
Unearned income	26,192	31,615	11,117	22,582	24,453	25,569 (average)
Donations and subsidies	35,185	46,010	38,619	48,870	62,267	41,963 (average)
Donations	32,972	42,977	35,876	45,694	57,029	39,180 (average)
Subsidies and other similar items	2,213	3,033	2,743	3,176	5,238	2,783 (average)
Rent and interest	−8,993	−14,395	−27,502	−26,288	−37,814	−16,394 (average)
Receipts	2,231	6,465	5,383	4,407	10,709	4,678 (average)
Expenditures	−11,224	−20,860	−32,885	−30,695	−48,523	−21,072 (average)
Rent	−7,457	−13,166	−22,066	−18,785	−24,381	−13,161 (average)
Interest	−3,767	−7,694	−10,819	−11,910	−24,142	−7,911 (average)
Taxes per household	5,888	13,068	18,019	25,904	37,700	13,041 (average)
Charges per household[c]	2,726	4,594	6,341	7,132	9,332	4,544 (average)
Per capita tax	1,107	2,045	2,425	3,084	4,368	2,038 (average)
Per acre tax	5,795	7,075	5,809	6,150	6,225	6,146 (average)
Per capita net income after tax and charges	51,811	64,049	66,494	72,548	95,248	62,563 (average)
Per capita net earned income after tax and charges	46,889	59,102	64,998	69,859	93,702	58,568 (average)
Per capita living expenditure per household	52,779	59,793	63,382	69,914	95,689	61,942 (average)
Per capita deficit or surplus with aids	−968	4,256	3,112	2,634	−441	621 (average)
Per family deficit or surplus without aids	−7,581	−2,944	−2,085	−3,184	−6,368	−5,936 (average)

[a] 60 farm districts.

[b] Total net income equals farming and nonfarming income minus farming and nonfarming cost.

[c] Nonrecurrent levies imposed by local government.

SOURCE: Bank of Korea, Research Department.

for outside aid. But it is important to note that among farms of the three middle sizes there is no substantial difference in the deficit: farmers with average holdings of 1.847, 3.102, and 4.212 acres have deficits of about 4.6, 3.3, and 4.9 per cent of living expenditures, respectively, excluding donations and subsidies.

There are, however, substantial differences in living expenditures between farmers with relatively small landholdings and those with large landholdings. The farmers with relatively larger holdings would not have a deficit if their living expenditures (per member of the family) were a little lower. But this is not true of farmers whose holdings are less than 3.102 acres, for their living standards are lower than the average, in fact too low to be acceptable. The annual per capita living expenditure of extremely poor farmers was, on the average, about $52 (at the free exchange rate) for farms averaging 1.016 acres, and about $59 for farms averaging 1.847 acres.

Thus the prospects for project financing by the agricultural community itself are very discouraging. This is accentuated by the fact that the net income of farm families does not even take into account any of the implicit costs incurred in farm operation. Wage costs for family labor and potential interest on their own capital are not subtracted from net income. Moreover, some surplus must be reserved, in the form of seeds and fertilizer, for the coming year's operation. Even by including donations and subsidies, the Korean farm household saved an average of only about 621 *hwan* in 1959. This is virtually zero saving. The picture is indeed pessimistic, but, nevertheless, all hope of finding ways of financing the proposed capital improvement projects by the agricultural community itself need not be relinquished.

SPECIFIC PROPOSALS FOR CREATING
A CAPITAL IMPROVEMENT FUND

A careful investigation of the present distribution of agricultural funds in the government budget, and of the land income tax in the farm family budget, leads to the following specific proposals: (1) subsidies now given to individual farm households by the government, in order to promote agricultural production, should instead be allocated to a fund for community capital improvement projects; (2) some of the net rent now paid to absentee landowners, which flows out of the rural community, should be retained for rural capital projects.

In connection with the first proposal it should be noted that current production and employment could not be sustained without donations and subsidies. Funds for both these aids must be kept within the agricultural community, but better use should be made of subsidy funds. Donations are goods and cash given to poor farmers by relatives, private persons, and charitable organizations, plus pensions and retirement allowances; these funds, as donations, are not available for community capital improvement. Subsidies are principally funds given by the government for encouraging agricultural production and for improving farming facilities. The amount given to each farm household (2,783 *hwan*, on the average), however, is too small to bring about any of the desired aims on an individual basis. Therefore, instead of distributing subsidies among farmers, it is here suggested that they be used in a lump sum for community capital improvement projects, such as the proposed farm-land development projects. For the entire sample of 582 farm households, the subsidies totaled about 1.6 million *hwan;* and for the entire agricultural community the total was about 6.279 million *hwan*.[8]

The rationale of the second proposal is nearly the same as that of land reform. Land reform has become an accepted social measure in underdeveloped societies. There is no need, therefore, to shy away from a rent tax that would bring about nearly the same effect as land reform without, perhaps, resulting in so much disturbance to the political *status quo*. The rent tax plan would result in the virtual extinction of absentee landownership and in the subsequent division of the land among tillers. As owner farming is economically preferable to tenant farming, this scheme would have a favorable effect on employment and production. Such a rent tax (over and above the income tax which includes current rent income) would also substantially reduce the price of land. In underdeveloped countries land prices are unduly

[8] To derive this figure, 2,256,161 farm households are taken as full-time farming units, and this number of farm households is multiplied by the average subsidy per household, or 2,783 *hwan*.

high as compared with land yield, so that the high price of land becomes one of the major factors in depressing the living scale of farmers.

Actually the announcement of such a rent tax scheme would cause furious land selling. The purchase of land from absentee owners would lower the price of land in Korea and there would be heavy selling and outflow of capital. But the government could step in and buy up the land with long-term government bonds, in order to prevent the outflow of this rural capital. The land thus acquired by the government would soon be divided among tillers, for a reasonable price, to be paid over a protracted period of time. The prevention of the outflow of capital from rural areas is an absolute necessity for the program here outlined. As the fund obtainable from this source is, in any event, comparatively small, a reasonably satisfactory compensation plan to absentee owners could be carried out within a very short period of time, say two years at the most. The price of the land acquired by tillers should also be determined according to the limit of actual incremental output.

As for the funds obtainable from this source, the Bank of Korea has calculated that the net rent outflow from rural areas has been 2,047 *hwan* per average farm household. From the whole rural community, approximately 4,618 million *hwan* could be made available by levying a tax on rent. As stated earlier in this chapter, the rationale of this rent tax is to retain the larger part of this income in the rural community, so that the fund to be used for capital projects would become an additional asset to the rural community, an asset originally created, in fact, by rural people themselves.

In passing, it should be stressed that receivers of land rent are frequently moneylenders. The scheme to tax land rents could, therefore, reduce the funds for loans necessary to poor farmers for the purchase of fertilizers, seeds, and other needed items. If the fund financed by the rent tax were to be used to increase employment through capital improvement projects, it would not be available for loans. This disappearance of capital for loans would be a serious blow to the struggling farmer. This problem would need a solution. Nevertheless, I advocate the creation and use of this fund for urgently needed capital improvement projects.

It should also be noted that the opportunity of using rent tax for economic development has recently declined to a large extent. Land rent had been considered a rich potential source of capital formation. It gradually became evident, however, that conspicuous consumption on the part of landlords constituted a major obstacle to a high level of capital formation. Partly for this reason, most Asian countries in recent times have undertaken a drastic transfer of landownership from absentee landlords to tillers. Recent land reforms in Korea (in 1948 and in 1950) appreciably reduced absentee landownership. As a result, the potential revenue from the rent tax alone cannot be expected to play a dramatic part in the economic development needed for the utilization of the underemployed within the agricultural community, but its role would not be insignificant.

A PROPOSAL FOR REPLACING THE LAND INCOME TAX WITH A LAND PROPERTY TAX

It is the goal of the program proposed in this chapter not only to show the way to the creation of a capital improvement fund financed by the agricultural community itself, but also, as an important part of the proposed program, to suggest a way further to alleviate the social and economic stagnation of rural society through a proposal for improving the agricultural organization. The rationale of this additional proposal is to create more intensive farming by replacing the land income tax with a land property tax. As income is the primary determinant of the scale of living, it has been regarded as the best measure of ability to pay taxes. The obsession with income as the measure of all economic activity and economic ability to pay taxes has already been extensively discussed in economic literature. Only one specific ramification, of particular relevance, will be discussed here.

The system of taxation on income discriminates against income from labor as compared with income from capital. As pointed out in chapter vi, the output per given unit of land is greater for the small farm than it is for the large farm. This difference is due primarily to the intensity of labor expended on the small farm. The extra income thus realized by the farmers of smaller holdings results from additional hard labor; this is not taken into account by the government in its tax rates, nor does the farmer of this smaller unit benefit from the revenue realized by the government from this disproportionate taxation. Additional intensive labor also requires additional consumption of food and other living expenditures; thus, the ability to pay income taxes may not be increased by the extra (gross) income. Either principle of taxation—the benefit principle or the ability principle—proves that the tax based on income, in rural Korea, discriminates against income from labor as compared with income from property.

Table 19 shows that the average income tax per acre on larger farms, 4.212 acres and up, is lower than the average per acre tax on a 1.847-acre farm. This is a regressive tax system.

What does this discriminatory and regressive tax system mean in terms of economic development? It means the prevalence of self-supporting family farming based on larger (less taxable) farms and larger families, which, in turn, means more tradition-directed underemployment, lower productivity per unit of land, little or no savings, and labor immobility. All these conditions, cumulatively, spell out greater socioeconomic stagnation.

A land property tax instead of a land income tax would be a significant help in solving these problems. Even if the total tax revenue would remain unchanged, and the land property tax distribution would be no different from the land income tax distribution, the land property tax would give added incentive to expend labor, and thus would result in a larger output, because this tax would not impede incremental output acquired by additional labor expended. Second, even a uniform land property tax would have a substantial and beneficial effect on the size of farm and the size of family: a strictly proportional land property tax would be a more progressive tax in terms of income. The increase in progressivity may not be substantial, but the marginal effect of the loss of income on the size of farm and family would be significant because the income of all taxpayers is in any event at a very low level. Third, the effects of such a tax would certainly create a preference for smaller holdings which, in turn, would contribute to smaller family groupings, and thus to an eventual breakup of a key traditional social institution. Consequently, the mobility and the volume of labor would increase. In the long run, a dynamic consequence would be that, as the urban industrial sector, as well as the rural sector, itself develops to a higher stage, the exodus of farmers to industrial areas would make it possible to realize a (new) optimum size of farm, larger than before. Such a dynamic process may stretch to the point where the outflow of capital from the rural area to urban industry may become economically practical.

The present land income tax is highly inconsistent with the land reform that the Korean government has been so eager to achieve.[9] The purpose of land reform is to give the land to tillers according to their ability to cultivate and to obtain a larger output via the system of small-owner farming. Nonetheless, the current land income tax tends to create a nonoptimum farm size. A land property tax, on the other hand, would increase employment and output, by the nontaxed (through income) intensiveness of labor, instead of decreasing them, as is true of the present land income tax. The use to which the land property tax would be put and its effects would significantly improve farm organization and farm production.

ESTIMATE OF LABOR MOBILIZABLE WITH THE PROPOSED CAPITAL IMPROVEMENT FUND

The next problem is to estimate the volume of labor that could be intermittently mobilized in off seasons with the fund obtained by the proposals here outlined. The fund obtainable from converting subsidies into earned income, according to calculations for 1959, is about 6,279 million *hwan,* and, from net land rent taxes, about 4,618 million *hwan.* All in all, the total available is about 10,897 million *hwan.* This is about 1.8 per cent of the total executed government expenditure of 608,723 million *hwan* in the same fiscal year (1959).[10] This may not seem large, but actually it represents about 51 per cent of the 21,563 million *hwan* in the government agricultural budget for fiscal 1959. Compared with the government revenue from agriculture (various taxes, in-

[9] There still remains some vested property to be distributed; and the payment for the land by the farmers has not yet been completed.

[10] The budget includes both general and special accounts. The latter includes, among others, a land reform management account. The farm-land development fund comes from both accounts.

terest on government loans to farmers, and other service charges),
this proposed fund amounts to about 52 per cent of the government agricultural revenue of about 21,000 million *hwan,* in the
same fiscal year.[11] It is approximately 53 per cent of the farm-
land development fund in 1958.[12] Thus the fund obtainable
through my proposals is, in fact, a substantial addition to agricultural capital formation.

Let us now use this fund to hire labor for capital improvements.
Let us assume that the average per capita living cost is 62,500
hwan,[13] including the extra 2,047 *hwan* made available to every
farm household by eliminating the rent formerly paid to absentee
landowners. On this basis, about 151,300 workers could be mobilized for our projects.[14] This amounts to approximately 57 per
cent of the total technical idle labor of 264,000 farm workers. As
there is no withdrawable labor in the peak agricultural months
of June, July, and October, the fund unused in these months may
be allocated to the other nine months. On this nine-month basis,
the total mobilizable labor would be about 189,000 workers, or
a little more than 71 per cent of the technical idle labor.[15]

As there are relatively few wage laborers in Korean agricultural
communities, this program would be applied mainly to farmers
with less than optimum holdings, that is, with an average land-

---

[11] In fiscal 1959 the land income tax was about 19,272 million *hwan.* The
budgetary figures are not exactly comparable with the sample data because the
crops collected in kind, as a tax, are valued at the budgetary prices in the budget,
whereas those in the sample data are valued at the local market prices. The two
prices are often substantially different.

[12] For the central government agricultural budget, see Bank of Korea, Research
Department, *Annual Economic Review,* 1959, sec. 1, pp. 96–97; for the farm-land
development fund, see *ibid.,* p. 45. The farm-land development fund came from two
sources: government subsidies and government long-term loans (about 10 and 11
million *hwan,* respectively).

[13] This is $\frac{1}{2}$ (72,000 + 53,000). The assumptions are: (1) the proportion of workers
and nonworkers is 1 to 1; (2) workers, including household workers, consume about
15 per cent more than the average level of 62,000 *hwan,* or about 40 per cent more
than nonworkers, on the average. Specifically, 62,500 (1 + 0.15) = 72,000; and 62,500
= $\frac{1}{2}$ (72,000 + x), where x equals the average consumption of nonworkers.

[14] The magnitude of mobilizable labor is computed by dividing the 10,897 million
hwan by the worker's consumption, 72,000 *hwan.*

[15] The mobilizable labor on a nine-month basis is computed as follows: The
laborer's consumption on a nine-month basis is 60,000 *hwan* (i.e., 72,000 × 9/12).
And the saving owing to the peak agricultural season amounts to 2,724 million
hwan (i.e., 10,897 million × 3/12). The balance of 8,173 million *hwan* will still be
sufficient to mobilize the same number of workers as before, about 151,300 persons;
and 2,724 million *hwan* can be used to mobilize about 37,800 workers. The total
mobilizable labor is therefore about 189,000 workers.

holding of less than 2 acres. Farmers with holdings of this size are quite dependent on additional earnings through wage employment, but they cannot, because of this, be called agricultural laborers per se.[16] Farmers with less than optimum holdings are idle in a technical sense and would therefore respond more readily to the program, because the remuneration from wage employment on capital projects, 72,000 *hwan* per worker per year, is larger than the current earnings of these small farmers.

On the other hand, farmers with small holdings who, as a result of the abolition of the land income tax, would be able to afford more food and keep more of their income, would still tend to accept wage employment outside their farms, because the remuneration on the capital improvement projects would be higher than their earnings even under the improved conditions brought about by the property land tax system. It is quite conceivable that farmers with small landholdings might decide to sell their farms and become wage laborers permanently. This would contribute to the creation of more optimum-size holdings, to increased savings, to increased surplus labor, to greater labor mobility—all prerequisites for economic progress in underdeveloped agricultural communities.

---

[16] In fact, the Bank of Korea considers that farmers with this size of holding could be called agricultural laborers, on the ground that they are frequently employed for wages on large estates or in rural construction work. The bank, however, overstates its case, for these farmers actually earned more than 74 per cent of their total income from self-employment on their land. About 14 per cent of their total earnings came from wages, and the rest, about 12 per cent, from donations and subsidies. For income data see appendix table 4; for the position of the bank on this matter, see Bank of Korea, Research Department, *Annual Economic Review,* 1959, sec. 1, p. 43.

IX

Summary Conclusions

The existing diversity of "diagnoses" and "remedies" offered to cure the "disorders" of manpower utilization in underdeveloped economies is, by and large, inapplicable to underdeveloped agricultural societies. Not all unutilized labor in these societies is surplus, nor is all the utilized labor nonsurplus. Most of these societies are tradition-directed, and in tradition-directed areas the supply of labor is not unlimited, as has been suggested by some economists; but, on the other hand, all the unemployment is not surplus, as has been suggested by David Riesman and others. In any event, it is indeed not true that, *ceteris paribus,* surplus labor is a mass phenomenon in backward and improverished, tradition-directed, rural communities.

Using Korea as a case example, we concluded that in a society in which traditional social institutions such as the extended-family–clan–village system play an important role in individual choice making, the scales tend to tip in favor of the existence of tradition-directed underemployment rather than of disguised unemployment, to the extent that conscious choices cause individuals to endure a miserable life, ridden by hunger and disease. Such customs and traditions inhibit economic motivation, block labor mobility, and limit private savings for technical and capital improvements. They are consequently strong deterrents to economic development. The people living in impoverished rural communities are, of course, economically not happy, but neither are they unhappy enough to break through the traditional social institutions. Tradition-directed underemployment in these circumstances is, in a sense, "closed," because it is voluntary and not withdrawable from the land without drastic social change and/or changes in the economy, such as the attraction of substantially higher earnings in alternative occupations. Without such changes, the only other alternative would be a totalitarian method for drawing tradition-directed underemployment from the land.

Underemployment in these economies is not, however, wholly tradition-directed. A notable example of this is seasonal underemployment of attached wageworkers. Seasonal underemployment exists, of course, in any agricultural economy insofar as the process of production by nature is not continuous and is beyond individual control. In this circumstance, idle labor may be seen as a technical matter; and the technically underemployed in poverty-stricken societies may be, not only economically but also socially, marginal individuals. This underemployment is therefore "open" in the sense that, *ceteris paribus,* it could be withdrawn from the land.

Marginal men are those who are most susceptible to making new adjustments in situations of change, owing to their marginal economic and social situations. Therefore, only the idle labor of marginal men may be considered as true surplus labor which can be removed from the land without creating problems. Self-supporting family workers are not socially marginal individuals because they are steeped in tradition and, by and large, prefer the security, the personal dignity, and the lack of imposed pressures which accompany landownership and self-employment. In this important sense, the idle labor of self-supporting family members cannot be regarded as true surplus labor. For these reasons, the conventional treatment of underemployment of self-supporting family labor as true surplus labor lacks analytical and empirical validity. In our model, underemployment, rather than unemployment, exists among tradition-directed farm labor. And only in the sense that this underemployment is closed and voluntary is it "disguised." This tradition-directed underemployment is not true surplus labor and is not withdrawable from the land, under the constraints of *ceteris paribus.*

On the other hand, self-supporting family workers may be economically marginal even though they are not socially marginal.

In such circumstances, the idle labor of self-supporting family workers may be partly technical and partly tradition-directed. We found that for the Korean agricultural community as a whole, about 30 per cent of the labor available was underemployed. Technical (or open) underemployment of 11 per cent included both self-supporting family and attached wage labor; the remaining 19 per cent of the total labor available was tradition-directed (or closed) underemployment. The 11 per cent represented 38 per cent of the total idle labor, and the 19 per cent represented 62 per cent of the total idle labor.

To arrive at a valid method of measuring surplus labor in backward agricultural economies, we had to discard the prevailing concepts and methods of estimating surplus labor, concepts and methods rooted in theories of "disguised unemployment." This key concept of disguised unemployment as surplus labor merely confuses the vital issue of manpower utilization in economically underdeveloped countries today. Its principal weaknesses, among others, are (1) the identification of technical (open) idle labor with tradition-directed (closed) underemployment; (2) the obscurity of the idea of marginal or zero productivity of labor actually working; (3) the confusion in dealing with wage labor and self-supporting family labor and in relating them to the estimate of surplus labor or disguised unemployment; and (4) the apparent underestimating and misunderstanding of the role that the tradition-directed institution of the extended family "dole" plays in employment and unemployment.

Our review and analysis of the literature on disguised unemployment led us to the conclusion that the term "disguised" in this context is largely meaningless or irrelevant. We contend that the term "disguised" has a valid meaning only in connection with the tradition-directed underemployment of self-supporting family workers; the social institutions in which this type of farm worker is steeped serve as a sort of veil over his actual employment condition and render "invisible" or "disguised" his state of underemployment. Only a social revolution would lift this veil and transform this closed underemployment into open unemployment. And marginal or zero productivity has nothing to do with the determination of the existence of this underemployment.

Our contentions with regard to the nature and volume of unutilized labor, in our case example of rural Korea, led us further to conclusions as to the best development program under the *ceteris paribus* constraints, and within the fact of the almost inevitable unavailability of additional capital. The development program that we proposed and the methods for financing it would not only put to work unutilized labor in much-needed rural capital improvement projects, but could also pave the way to the gradual dissolution of those traditions and institutions that contribute so heavily to the economic stagnation of a typical underdeveloped rural community.

Because of the very low capital-output ratio, and because the social cost of employing idle farm labor near the villages is negligible, we gave farm-land development projects first priority for investment. The unavailability of capital from other sectors of the economy led us to find specific methods for raising funds from the agricultural community itself, using subsidy funds in a lump sum for development projects, and imposing a land rent tax on land rented out to tenant farmers by absentee owners.

To put a premium on intense labor and thus increase production, we proposed the substitution of a land property tax for the land income tax. This could also help promote the optimum size of farm holdings.

Our proposals for utilizing idle labor and promoting economic progress in the agricultural community generally would be less disturbing to the political *status quo* than outright confiscation and redistribution of land; than forceful, totalitarian methods of withdrawing tradition-directed labor from the land; or than other methods for the utilization of idle labor and for economic development in violation of *ceteris paribus* constraints.

Appendix

APPENDIX TABLE 1

MAN-HOURS EMPLOYED BY TYPE OF FARMING, AVERAGE PER HOUSEHOLD, KOREA,[a] 1959

(In hours, unconverted)

Month	Grand total[b]	Own farming							Other farming			
		Subtotal[b]	Rice cultivation	Summer grain cultivation	Other cultivation	Sericulture	Animal husbandry	Others	Subtotal[b]	Wage labor	Compulsory labor	Others
January	144.37	64.49	2.04	9.88	2.43	0.17	5.23	44.74	79.89	8.86	0.41	70.62
February	74.92	37.39	0.05	9.17	2.55	0.10	5.36	20.16	37.53	5.33	0.30	31.91
March	249.14	158.53	11.36	75.14	17.77	0.85	5.44	47.96	90.62	19.87	7.69	63.05
April	251.31	156.44	51.52	31.33	22.56	1.07	10.41	39.55	94.87	20.09	5.48	69.30
May	292.73	209.37	74.76	13.39	38.70	3.72	19.52	59.28	83.36	27.03	2.65	53.68
June	496.17	415.62	189.25	112.62	71.17	3.66	13.83	25.09	80.55	64.05	1.87	14.63
July	411.59	357.27	138.54	7.25	132.52	2.29	20.21	56.46	54.32	43.36	1.41	9.55
August	291.95	240.07	49.27	1.52	65.24	0.22	25.40	98.42	51.88	18.54	1.58	31.76
September	244.75	165.31	23.40	0.31	48.67	4.14	24.04	64.75	79.44	10.08	3.66	65.70
October	449.90	360.17	180.69	48.00	71.63	0.22	10.22	49.41	89.73	48.01	1.49	40.23
November	270.23	163.20	43.68	22.02	28.87	0.01	6.99	61.63	107.04	30.03	1.07	75.94
December	161.57	69.74	1.71	6.27	4.26	—	8.58	48.92	91.84	14.85	0.39	76.60
Total[b]	3,338.64	2,397.59	766.27	336.90	506.37	16.45	155.23	616.37	941.08	310.10	28.00	602.98

[a] 60 farm districts.

[b] Because of rounding, individual figures do not necessarily add up to total.

SOURCE: Bank of Korea, Research Department, *Economic Statistics Year Book*, 1960, pp. 300–301.

APPENDIX TABLE 2

MAN-HOURS EMPLOYED IN FARMING, AVERAGE PER HOUSEHOLD, KOREA,[a] 1959

(In hours, unconverted)

Month	Total[b]	Family labor employed						Male and female[b]	Wage labor employed					
		Male			Female				Attached			Casual		
		14 and under	15-59	60 and above	14 and under	15-59	60 and above		Male 15-59	Female 15-59	Male and female[b]	Male 15-59	Female 15-59	Male and female[b]
January	144.37	0.50	86.13	3.60	0.31	32.36	3.70	126.60	13.08	0.56	13.63	2.93	1.21	4.14
February	74.92	0.32	45.08	1.74	0.19	15.87	1.50	64.69	6.42	0.30	6.72	2.96	0.55	3.51
March	249.14	1.93	124.76	4.78	1.06	66.76	3.50	202.81	18.64	1.10	19.73	16.59	10.01	26.59
April	251.31	1.10	135.93	5.71	0.56	54.74	2.82	200.86	25.30	0.84	26.14	17.93	6.38	24.31
May	292.73	2.13	159.71	7.55	0.67	58.55	3.65	232.24	32.37	1.34	33.71	23.12	3.66	26.78
June	496.17	3.26	219.44	11.55	1.76	107.75	5.77	349.53	34.85	0.41	35.26	76.82	34.56	111.38
July	411.59	2.35	186.86	9.72	1.25	106.07	6.49	312.74	31.11	0.23	31.34	49.48	18.03	67.51
August	291.95	3.23	155.94	7.32	1.49	75.46	4.86	248.30	27.55	—	27.55	11.68	4.42	16.10
September	244.75	2.03	137.69	6.85	1.27	56.71	5.06	209.61	23.50	0.14	23.64	8.60	2.90	11.50
October	449.90	2.11	216.96	13.49	2.23	95.62	5.47	335.88	33.52	0.52	34.04	69.09	10.89	79.98
November	270.23	0.33	147.35	8.25	0.90	49.07	3.41	209.31	25.94	0.24	26.19	27.22	7.51	34.74
December	161.57	0.71	98.07	3.49	3.71	30.95	2.26	139.19	16.18	0.32	16.50	4.46	1.43	5.89
Total[b]	3,338.64	20.00	1,713.92	84.03	15.41	749.91	48.49	2,631.76	288.46	6.00	294.47	310.88	101.54	412.42

[a] 60 farm districts.

[b] Because of rounding, individual figures do not necessarily add up to total.

SOURCE: Bank of Korea, Research Department, *Economic Statistics Year Book*, 1960, pp. 300-301.

APPENDIX TABLE 3

Capital Stock, Average per Household, Korea,[a] 1959

Item	Unit of measure- ment	Average	Size of farm (in acres)				
			1.225 and under	1.225– 2.450	2.450– 3.675	3.675– 4.900	4.900 and above
Land	*Pyong*[b]	4,486	1,715	3,186	8,911	12,356	14,079
Dry fields	*Pyong*	812	413	736	1,238	1,607	2,624
Paddy fields	*Pyong*	1,591	763	1,431	2,435	3,497	4,999
Mulberry fields	*Pyong*	5	1	3	3	28	28
Forests	*Pyong*	1,949	460	910	5,083	6,917	5,989
Others	*Pyong*	129	78	106	152	307	409
Buildings	*Pyong*	24.75	18.91	25.63	27.32	37.31	46.20
Farm implements							
Kerosene engines	Each	0.01	0.00	0.01	—	0.04	0.08
Diesel engines	Each	0.02	0.02	0.02	0.01	0.02	—
Ploughs and harrows	Each	0.98	0.54	0.96	1.54	2.00	1.76
Pumps	Each	0.00	—	—	0.01	0.06	—
Fans	Each	0.04	0.02	0.03	0.05	0.06	0.24
Winnowers	Each	0.08	0.03	0.07	0.11	0.25	0.20
Straw rope twisters	Each	0.07	0.02	0.06	0.11	0.23	0.20
Straw bag twisters	Each	0.21	0.16	0.20	0.29	0.32	0.40
Sprayers	Each	0.05	0.01	0.04	0.09	0.23	0.16
Grain cleaning machines	Each	0.05	0.02	0.03	0.01	0.06	0.60
Threshers	Each	0.41	0.24	0.36	0.58	0.87	0.88
Carts	Each	0.08	0.02	0.09	0.14	0.30	0.24
Bicycles	Each	0.05	0.03	0.05	0.22	0.19	0.24
Others	Each	0.40	0.21	0.40	0.59	0.59	0.72
Trees and vines	*Hwan*[c]	9,307	4,735	8,161	8,291	29,934	28,243
Domestic animals							
Cattle	Each	0.41	0.21	0.41	0.63	0.77	1.08
Horses	Each	0.01	0.01	0.01	—	0.04	—
Pigs	Each	0.70	0.59	0.70	0.78	0.09	0.96
Sheep	Each	0.03	0.02	0.02	0.03	0.13	0.04
Honey bees	Hive	0.10	0.09	0.08	0.05	0.30	—
Stocked agricultural products	*Hwan*	173,628	88,656	162,521	257,203	354,359	511,072
Production materials	*Hwan*	11,239	6,564	11,175	16,836	19,736	26,036
Cash and quasi cash	*Hwan*	19,226	13,535	17,764	24,974	37,475	35,688
Cash	*Hwan*	7,519	5,531	7,001	9,258	8,465	24,330
Deposits	*Hwan*	626	310	503	1,459	660	2,121
Loans	*Hwan*	4,450	2,848	4,405	7,184	9,702	2,800
Others	*Hwan*	6,632	4,846	5,854	7,073	18,648	6,436
Total assets	1,000 hwan	1,456	739	1,305	2,178	3,265	4,221
Debts	*Hwan*	39,933	18,141	46,389	53,436	67,634	120,340
Individuals	*Hwan*	18,341	12,224	30,001	32,508	29,351	29,440
Banks	*Hwan*	14,238	5,079	14,212	19,300	32,196	57,960
Government and public financial institutions	*Hwan*	1,072	75	774	—	2,660	13,600
Others	*Hwan*	6,281	763	1,402	1,628	3,427	19,340
Net assets	1,000 hwan	1,417	720	1,259	2,125	3,198	4,101

[a] 60 farm districts, 582 farms.
[b] Approximately 1,225 *pyong* = 1 acre.
[c] 1 *hwan* = approximately 1 dollar.
NOTE: Individual figures do not necessarily add up to group totals.
SOURCE: Bank of Korea, Research Department, *Economic Statistics Year Book*, 1960, pp. 292–295.

APPENDIX TABLE 4

FARMERS' INCOME, AVERAGE PER HOUSEHOLD, KOREA,[a] 1959

			Size of farm (in acres)					
			1.225 and under	1.225–2.450	2.450–3.675	3.675–4.900	4.900 and above	Average
Size of sample			227	194	81	46	34	b
Average size of family			5.32	6.39	7.43	8.40	8.63	6.40
Cultivated land (in acres)			1,016	1,847	3,102	4,212	6,056	2,122
Farming proceeds (in *hwan*)	Proceeds in cash and kind	1	242,027	377,018	575,239	681,576	1,013,658	411,645
	Increase or decrease of stocks	2	−15,906	1,528	−19,223	17,496	−19,786	−13,603
	Increase or decrease of animals and trees	3	17,788	37,291	35,553	41,109	56,475	27,824
	Total (1 + 2 + 3)	4	243,909	415,837	591,569	740,181	1,050,347	425,866
Farming cost (in *hwan*)	Materials	5	55,226	81,378	117,342	133,940	202,826	87,250
	Wages, charges, and rentals	6	18,327	35,940	71,116	88,124	145,477	44,103
	Increase or decrease of stock materials	7	−1,844	−4,397	−7,473	−6,272	−839	−3,524
	Total (5 + 6 + 7)	8	71,709	112,921	180,985	215,792	347,464	127,829
Gross farming profits (4–8)		9	172,200	302,916	410,584	524,389	702,884	298,037
Nonfarming proceeds		10	44,814	58,180	59,537	61,206	110,485	56,554
Nonfarming expenditures		11	5,820	19,508	13,155	18,489	31,067	13,847
Gross nonfarming profits (10–11)		12	38,994	38,672	46,382	42,717	79,418	42,707
Receipts from donations and subsidies		13	35,185	46,010	38,619	48,870	62,267	41,963
Receipts from wages, salaries, rentals, and interest		14	37,874	39,338	22,827	26,461	35,569	35,281
Gross farm income (9 + 12 + 13 + 14)		15	284,253	426,936	518,412	642,437	880,137	417,988
Taxes and charges		16	8,614	17,662	24,360	33,036	47,073	17,585
Farm income after taxes and charges (15–16)		17	275,639	409,274	494,052	609,401	833,064	400,403
Living expenditures		18	280,784	382,084	470,931	587,275	825,803	396,430
Engel's coefficient			58.8	54.1	53.4	53.3	50.8	54.7
Surplus or deficit (17–18)			−5,145	27,190	23,121	22,126	7,261	3,973

[a] 60 farm districts.
[b] Total size of sample = 582.
SOURCE: Bank of Korea, Research Department, *Economic Statistics Year Book*, 1960, p. 278.

APPENDIX TABLE 5

GRAIN CONTROL BY KOREAN GOVERNMENT, 1958
(In *suk*,[a] polished)

	Rice	Other	Total
Armed forces	1,283,000	346,000	1,629,000
Government officials	—	1,464,000	1,464,000
Prisoners	28,000	28,000	56,000
Grain loan	—	500,000	500,000
Seeding	60,000	52,000	112,000
Market control	41,000	629,000	670,000
Reserve stock	—	750,000	750,000
Total	1,412,000	3,769,000	5,181,000
Transferred grain from previous year	112,000	163,000	275,000
Rice collection	1,200,000	—	1,200,000
Land acquisition tax	900,000	—	900,000
Land repayment grain	200,000	—	200,000
Repayment from grain loan	100,000	—	100,000
Summer grain collection[b]	—	340,000	340,000
Land acquisition tax	—	160,000	160,000
Land repayment grain	—	30,000	30,000
Repayment from grain loan	—	150,000	150,000
Exchanged grain with fertilizer	100,000	—	100,000
Purchased grain	—	—	—
Imported grain	—	3,266,000	3,266,000
Total supply	1,412,000	3,769,000	5,181,000

[a] 1 *suk* = 4.96 bushels.
[b] Summer grains are barley, wheat, millet, and so forth.
SOURCE: Korea, Ministry of Agriculture and Forestry, *Year Book of Agriculture and Forestry*, 1959, p. 223.

Bibliography

"Agricultural Labour. I. Pattern of Occupation and Employment," *Economic Weekly*, VII (Aug., 1955).

Bancroft, Gertrude. "Current Unemployment Statistics of the Census Bureau and Some Alternatives," in *The Measurement and Behavior of Unemployment*. Conference of the Universities. Princeton: Princeton University Press, 1957.

Bhatnagar, Kalka P., *et al. Indian Rural Economy*. Parade-Kanpur: Kishore Publishing House, 1955.

Bhattacharjee, J. P., ed. "Employment of Manpower in Agriculture," in *Studies in Indian Agricultural Economics*. Bombay: Indian Society of Agricultural Economics, 1958.

Brinkmann, Carl. "Family. Social Aspects," *Encyclopaedia of the Social Sciences*, ed. Edwin R. A. Seligman and Alvin Johnson. Vol. VI. New York: Macmillan, 1931.

Buchanan, Norman S., and H. S. Ellis. *Approaches to Economic Development*. New York: Twentieth Century Fund, 1955.

Buck, John Lossing. *Chinese Farm Economy*. Chicago: University of Chicago Press, 1930.

———. *Land Utilization in China*. Chicago: University of Chicago Press, 1937.

Campbell, Bryam. *Race and Social Revolutions: Twenty-one Essays on Social Problems*. New York: Truth Seeker Company, 1958.

Chenery, Hollis B. "The Application of Investment Criteria," *Quarterly Journal of Economics*, LXVII (Feb. 1953).

Chiang, Hsieh. "Underemployment in Asia. I. Nature and Extent," *International Labour Review*, LXV (June, 1952).

Cho, Dong-Phil. "Agricultural Problems in Korea Today," *Korea Quarterly*, I (Autumn, 1959).

Cleland, Wendell W. *The Population Problem in Egypt: A Study of Population Trends and Conditions in Modern Egypt.* Lancaster, Pa.: Science Press Printing Co., 1936.

Deutsche, Gertrude. "How the Unemployed Are Counted," *Business Record* (Dec., 1960).

Ducoff, Louis J., and Margaret J. Hagood. *Labor Force Definition and Measurement: Recent Experience in the United States.* Social Science Research Council, Bulletin no. 56. New York, 1947.

Eckaus, R. S. "The Factor Proportions Problem in Underdeveloped Areas," *American Economic Review,* XLV (Sept., 1955).

Food and Agriculture Organization of the United Nations. *Food Balance Sheet.* 2d issue. Rome, 1955.

————. *Rehabilitation and Development of Agriculture, Forestry and Fisheries, in South Korea.* New York, 1954.

————. *Review of Food Consumption Survey.* Rome, 1958.

Frankel, H. "The Industrialization of Agricultural Countries and the Possibilities of a New International Division of Labor," *Economic Journal,* LIII (June-Sept., 1943).

Friedman, Milton. "The Methodology of Positive Economics," in *Essays in Positive Economics.* Chicago: University of Chicago Press, 1953.

Fukuoka, Masao. "Full Employment and Constant Coefficients of Production," *Quarterly Journal of Economics,* LXIX (Feb., 1955).

Galenson, W., and A. Zellner. *International Comparison of Unemployment Rates.* Reprint no. 86. Institute of Industrial Relations, University of California. Berkeley, 1957.

Georgescu-Roegen, N. "Economic Theory and Agrarian Economics," *Oxford Economic Papers,* XII (Feb., 1960).

Hamilton, Angus. *Korea.* New York: Charles Scribner's Sons, 1904.

Hamilton, Angus, *et al. Korea: Its History, Its People, and Its Commerce.* Oriental Series, XIII. Boston and Tokyo: J. B. Millet Co., 1910.

Harris, Marshall, and Robert A. Rohwer. *Family Farming.* National Planning Association, Washington. Planning Pamphlet no. 99. July, 1957.

Hertz, Frederich O. *The Economic Problem of the Danubian States: A Study in Economic Nationalism.* London: Victor Gollancz, 1947.

Higgins, Benjamin. *Economic Development: Principles, Problems, and Policies.* New York: W. W. Norton & Co., 1959.

Hoselitz, Berthold F. *Sociological Aspects of Economic Growth.* New York: Free Press of Glencoe, 1960.

Howard, Louise E. *Labour in Agriculture: An International Survey.*

Royal Institute of International Affairs. London: Oxford University Press, 1935.

India. Ministry of Labour. *Agricultural Labour Enquiry: Report on Intensive Survey of Agricultural Labour.* Vol. I. Delhi, 1955.

Indian Society of Agricultural Economics. "Employment of Manpower in Agriculture," in *Studies in Indian Agricultural Economics,* ed. J. P. Bhattacharjee. Bombay, 1958.

International Labour Office. *Conditions of Employment of Agricultural Workers.* Fourth Conference of American States Members of the International Labour Organization. Report III. Geneva, 1949.

———. *The Economic Background of Social Policy, Including Problems of Industrialization.* Preparatory Asiatic Regional Conference of the International Labour Organization. Report IV. New Delhi, 1947.

———. *Labor Problems in Agriculture.* International Labour Conference. Thirty-third session. Report VI. Geneva, 1950.

———. *The Second Conference of Labor Statistics.* Geneva, 1925.

———. *The Sixth International Conference of Labor Statistics.* Geneva, 1948.

Issawi, Charles P. *Egypt: An Economic and Social Analysis.* Royal Institute of International Affairs. London: Oxford University Press, 1947.

Kenadjian, Berdj. "Disguised Unemployment in Underdevelopd Countries." Unpublished Ph.D. dissertation, Harvard University, 1957.

Keynes, John M. *The General Theory of Employment, Interest and Money.* New York: Harcourt, Brace, 1936.

Klein, Sidney. *The Pattern of Land Tenure Reform in East Asia after World War II.* New York: Bookman Associates, 1958.

Koestner, N. "Some Comments on Professor Nurkse's Capital Accumulation in Underdeveloped Countries," *L'Egypte Contemporaine,* XLIV (April, 1953).

Korea. Bank of Korea. Research Department. *Annual Economic Review.* 1959. Seoul, 1959.

———. *Economic Statistics Year Book.* 1960. Seoul, 1960.

———. Headquarters Joint Military Staff. *Analysis of Korean Economy.* Seoul: Dong-Hwa Publishing Co., 1959.

———. Korean Agricultural Bank. Research Department. *Agricultural Year Book.* 1959, 1960. Seoul, 1959, 1960.

———. Korean Reconstruction Bank. *Economic Review.* 1945–1955. Seoul, 1955.

———. Ministry of Agriculture and Forestry. *Year Book of Agriculture and Forestry.* 1959, 1960. Seoul: 1959, 1960.

————. Ministry of Finance. Bureau of Taxation. *Year Book of Tax Statistics. 1959.* Seoul, 1959.

————. Ministry of Reconstruction. *Economic Survey. 1959.* Seoul, 1959.

Lamartine Yates, P., and D. Warriner. *Food and Farming in Post-War Europe.* London: Oxford University Press, 1943.

Lee, C. Y. *The Framework and Structure of the Korean Economy.* Social Sciences and Humanities Research Center of Korea. Korean Studies Series, II. Seoul, 1958.

Lee, Hoon Koo. *Land Utilization and Rural Economy in Korea.* Chicago: University of Chicago Press, 1936.

Leibenstein, Harvey. *Economic Backwardness and Economic Growth: Studies in the Theory of Economic Development.* New York: John Wiley & Sons, 1960.

Lewis, W. A. "Economic Development with Unlimited Supplies of Labour," *Manchester School of Economic and Social Studies,* XXII (May, 1954).

————. "Unlimited Labour: Further Notes," *Manchester School of Economic and Social Studies,* XXVI (Jan., 1958).

McCune, George M. *Korea Today.* Cambridge: Harvard University Press, 1950.

McCune, Shannon B. *Korea's Heritage: A Regional and Social Geography.* Rutland, Vt., and Tokyo: Charles E. Tuttle Co., 1956.

McKean, Roland N. *Efficiency in Government through Systems Analysis: With Emphasis on Water Resources Development.* New York: John Wiley & Sons, 1958.

Mazumdar, Dipak. "The Marginal Productivity Theory of Wages and Disguised Unemployment," *Review of Economic Studies,* XXVI (June, 1959).

Mazumdar, N. A. "Some Aspects of Underemployment," *Indian Economic Journal,* V (July, 1957).

Meier, Gerald M., and Robert E. Baldwin. *Economic Development: Theory, History, Policy.* New York: John Wiley & Sons, 1957.

Meier, Richard L. *Science and Economic Development: New Patterns of Living.* New York: John Wiley & Sons, 1956.

Moore, Wilbert E. *Economic Demography of Eastern and Southern Europe.* Geneva: League of Nations, 1945.

————. *Industrialization and Labor: Social Aspects of Economic Development.* Ithaca: Cornell University Press, 1951.

————. *Industrial Relations and the Social Orders.* Rev. ed. New York: Macmillan, 1951.

Mukerjee, Radhakamal. *The Institutional Theory of Economics.* London: Macmillan, 1942.

———. *Man and His Habitation: A Study in Social Ecology.* London and New York: Longmans, Green, 1940.

———. *The Rural Economy of India.* London: Longmans, Green, 1926.

Nanavati, Manilal B., and J. J. Anjaria. *The Indian Rural Problem.* 3d ed. Indian Society of Agricultural Economics. Bombay: Vora & Co., 1947.

Nasu, Shiroshi. *Land Utilization in Japan.* Chicago: University of Chicago Press, 1929.

Navarrete, Alfredo, Jr., and Ifigenia M. de Navarrete. "Underemployment in Underdeveloped Economies," in *The Economics of Underdevelopment,* ed. A. N. Agarwala and S. P. Singh. Bombay: Oxford University Press, 1958.

Nelson, Melvin F. *Korea and the Old Orders in Eastern Asia.* Baton Rouge: Louisiana State University Press, 1945.

Nurkse, Ragnar. *Problems of Capital Formation in Underdeveloped Countries.* Oxford: Basil Blackwell, 1955.

Park, Robert E. *Race and Culture.* Chicago: Free Press of Glencoe, 1950.

Pepper, Stephen C. *A Digest of Purposive Values.* Berkeley and Los Angeles: University of California Press, 1947.

Prest, Alan R. *War Economics of Primary Producing Countries.* Cambridge: Cambridge University Press, 1948.

"Promotion of Handicrafts in North Africa, The," *International Labour Review,* LXXVII (Jan., 1958).

Raj, K. N. "Employment and Unemployment in the Indian Economy: Problems of Classification, Measurement, and Policy," *Economic Development and Cultural Change,* VII (April, 1959).

———. *Employment Aspects of Planning in Underdeveloped Economies.* National Bank of Egypt. Fiftieth Anniversary Commemoration Lecture. Cairo, 1957.

"Reconsolidation of Holdings in Germany," *International Labour Review,* XXV (May, 1932).

Reserve Bank Rural Credit Survey Team, "Surplus Labour in Agriculture: Has It Been Sized Up?" *Economic Weekly,* VII (Aug., 1955).

Riesman, David, *et al., The Lonely Crowd: A Study of the Changing American Character.* New Haven: Yale University Press, 1950.

Robinson, Joan. *Essays in the Theory of Employment.* 2d ed. Oxford: Basil Blackwell, 1947.

Rochester, Anna. *Why Farmers Are Poor: The Agricultural Crisis in the United States*. New York: International Publishers, 1940.

Rosenstein-Rodan, P. N. "Disguised Unemployment and Underemployment in Agriculture," *Monthly Bulletin of Agricultural Economics and Statistics*, VI (July-Aug., 1957).

———. "Problems of Industrialization of Eastern and South-Eastern Europe," *Economic Journal*, LIII (June-Sept., 1943).

Sarkar, N. K., and S. J. Tambiah. *The Disintegrating Village*. Report of Social-Economic Survey Conducted by the University of Ceylon. Part 1. Colombo: Ceylon University Press Board, 1957.

Song, Chong-Keuk. "Some Food Problems in Korea," in *Theses Collection*. Vol. IV. Seoul: Chungang University, 1959.

Starcs, Peteris. "The Shortage of Agricultural Labour in Latvia," *International Labour Review*, XL (Dec., 1939).

Stonequist, Everett V. *The Marginal Man: A Study in Personality and Culture Conflict*. New York: Charles Scribner's, 1937.

Sung, Chang Hwan. *Economics of Korea*. Seoul: Jang Wang Sa, 1957.

Suriyakumaran, Canaganayagam. *The Economics of Full Employment in Agricultural Countries, with Special Reference to India and Ceylon*. Colombo: De Silva, 1957.

Talas, Cahit. "Handicrafts in Turkey," *International Labour Review*, LXXX (Oct., 1959).

Thorner, Daniel. "The Agricultural Labour Enquiry: Reflections on Concepts and Methods," *Economic Weekly*, XIII (June, 1956).

Thorner, Daniel and Alice. "Agricultural Manpower in India: Labourers," *Economic Weekly*, IX (Nov., 1957).

Tremelloni, Roberto. "The Parliamentary Inquiry into Unemployment in Italy," *International Labour Review*, LXVIII (Sept., 1953).

United Nations. Department of Economic Affairs. *Land Reform: Defects in Agrarian Structure as Obstacles to Economic Development*. New York, 1951.

———. ———. *Measures for the Economic Development of Underdeveloped Countries*. New York, 1951.

———. ———. Economic Commission for Asia and the Far East. *Economic Survey of Asia and the Far East, 1950*. New York, 1951.

United States. Department of State. Economic Commission. *Land Reform in Korea*. Seoul, 1947.

Van Der Kroef, Justus Maria. *Indonesian Social Evolution: Some Psychological Considerations*. Amsterdam: Wereld-Bibliotheek, 1958.

Viner, Jacob. "Some Reflections on the Concept of 'Disguised Unemployment,'" *Indian Journal of Economics*, XXXVIII (July, 1957).

Warriner, Doreen. *Economics of Peasant Farming.* London: Oxford University Press, 1939.

Wolf, Charles, Jr., and Sidney C. Sufrin. *Capital Formation and Foreign Investment in Underdeveloped Areas.* Maxwell School Series. Syracuse: Syracuse University Press, 1958.

"Women's Employment in Asian Countries," *International Labour Review,* LXVIII (Sept., 1953).

Wonnacott, Paul. "Disguised and Overt Unemployment in Underdeveloped Countries," *Quarterly Journal of Economics,* LXXVI (May., 1962).

————. *Land and Poverty in the Middle East.* Royal Institute of International Affairs. Middle East Economic and Social Studies. London, 1948.

Zensho, Eisuke. *Chosen no Jinko Kensyo* [*Population Phenomena of Korea*]. Chosa Siryo, no. 22. Seoul: Chosen-So-Tokoo-Hoo [Chosen Publishing Co.], 1927.

————. *Sei-Katsu, Cho-Tai Cho-Sa* [*Living Conditions Inquiry*]. Chosa Siryo, nos. 28–29, 32, 38–39, 40–41. Seoul: Chosen-So-Tokoo-Hoo [Chosen Publishing Co.], 1931, 1933, 1934, 1935.

Index